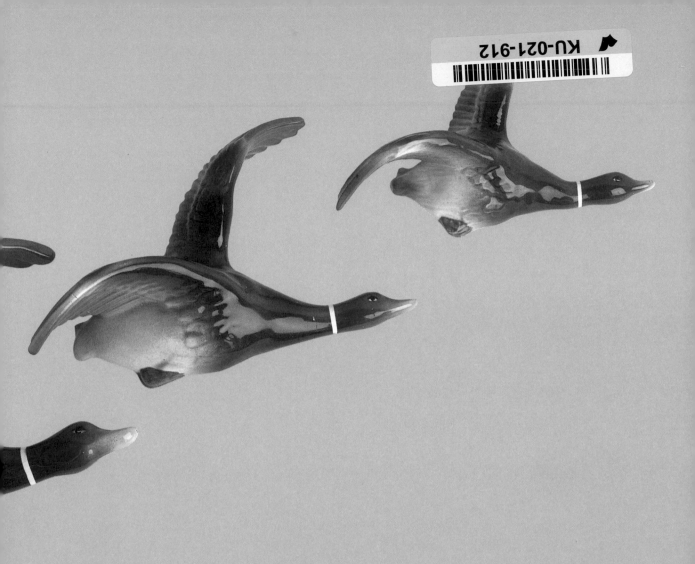

Miller's
Collecting the 1950s

To Jon, my favourite thing from the fifties

First published in Great Britain in 1997
by Miller's, an imprint of Reed Books Limited,
Michelin House, 81 Fulham Road, London SW3 6RB
and Auckland, Melbourne, Singapore and Toronto

Miller's is a registered trademark of
Reed International Books Limited

© 1997 Reed International Books Limited

Executive Editor Alison Starling
Executive Art Editor Vivienne Brar
Editor Nina Sharman
Designer Nina Pickup
Photographic coordinator Francesca Collin
Picture Research Wendy Gay
Production Jilly Sitford

Special photography Tim Ridley, Ian Booth and Robin Saker

The publishers will be grateful for any information which will assist them in
keeping future editions up to date. Although all reasonable care has been taken
in the preparation of this book, neither the publishers nor the compilers
can accept any liability for any consequence arising from the use thereof,
or the information contained herein.

A CIP record for this book is available from the British Library

ISBN 1 85732 887 6

Produced by Mandarin Offset
Printed and bound in Singapore

Miller's
Collecting the 1950s

Madeleine Marsh

MILLER'S

Contents

Introduction

My first encounter with the 1950s was a dressing-up box filled with my mother's cast-offs: billowing skirts decorated with blue roses and Parisian café scenes, multicoloured net petticoats that stood up all by themselves and veiled hats shaped like flowers As a child, these garments gave me a sense of pleasure that I have never lost. I still enjoy dressing up in 1950s style, and for me the fashions epitomize the most attractive features of period design: bold shapes, bright colours, brave patterns and, above all, sheer exuberance and a sense of fun.

This book is both a practical collector's guide, listing current market values, what to look out for and where to buy, and an unashamed celebration of the 1950s. It begins by going into the 1950s home and looks at everything from new designs in living-room furniture to the latest kitchen appliances. The second section uncovers fashion from evening clothes to underwear and the book concludes with 1950s leisure, from children's toys, to teenage rock 'n' roll, to adult reading.

The objects illustrated are hugely disparate, including serious and costly designer creations and the most bizarre extravagances of cheerful mass-produced kitsch: Charles Eames' furniture is shown along with plastic cocktail shakers shaped like pin-up girls; Dior dresses with circle-stitch bras; and Elvis Presley with Cliff Richard records. Items come from around the world, encompass a huge variety of media and were created for every taste and every pocket. What they have in common is their delight in exploring the new and a sense of extravagant liberation from the constraints and austerity of wartime subsistence. They are also united by their growing desirability in today's market.

The best 1950s material is now being granted "antique" status by the major auction houses, where, to the bemusement of experts in more traditional subjects, post-war plastic chairs are sold alongside 18th-century mahogany commodes. The pioneering designers of the period are the 20th-century heirs of the great craftsmen of the past, and their classic creations fetch high prices. In many fields values have doubled in the past five years and are still rising. However, antique shops, auction houses and dealers all have their own price ranges and you should use *Collecting the 50s* only as a guide. The price guides are for what you should expect to pay for items featured, not what you could sell them for to a dealer.

At the other end of the collecting scale, 1950s objects can still be picked up for very little from flea markets and second-hand shops, to say nothing of what lies forgotten in the attics of family homes. It is only comparatively recently that this material has become collectable. Much was simply thrown out when fashions changed and a great deal has still to be to be discovered. For the moment at least, products created for the mass market remain inexpensive, and collectors can still find designer pieces for junk shop prices.

A growing number of dealers and private collectors are becoming interested in the period and one of the most enjoyable aspects of researching this guide has been meeting some of them. The 1950s was an exciting and creative decade and seems to attract collectors and enthusiasts with similar qualities. People kindly allowed us to photograph their collections, were generous with their knowledge; and their enthusiasm has stimulated my own. My thanks to them for sharing. I had a lot of fun writing this book and I hope that you enjoy reading it.

The Royal Festival Hall at Night (1951), from a watercolour drawing by Maurice Wilson

1950 1951

Chronology

- Senator McCarthy launches his anti-Communist crusade, alleging the in-filtration of 205 communists into US State Department
- End of petrol and soap rationing in UK
- BBC radio serial *The Archers* an "every day story of country folk" launched.
- First kidney transplant in the USA
- X certificate introduced for films
- Outbreak of the Korean War, UN and Chinese troops become involved
- Russia announces it has an Atom bomb
- Andy Pandy launches *Watch with Mother* on BBC Television
- Uraguay wins the World Cup
- Diners Club issues its first credit cards
- UK chemical giant ICI launch wonder fabric Terylene
- First appearance of Charles M. Schulz' cartoon strip, *Peanuts*

- Festival of Britain – Royal Festival Hall, a permanent exhibition pavillion, is built on the South Bank site
- Labour government cuts meat ration to its lowest level ever, equivalent to 4oz (113gm) of steak per week
- Conservatives win election – Winston Churchill reinstalled as Prime Minister
- First Miss World contest
- First commercial manufacture of computers
- *A Street-Car Named Desire* popularizes Marlon Brando and the "scratch and mumble style" of method acting
- In the US, Julius and Ethel Rosenberg are sentenced to death for espionage; British diplomats Guy Burgess and Donald MacLean defect to the USSR
- Reported sightings of the Abominable Snowman in the Himalayas
- BBC Radio launches *Listen with Mother* with the unforgetable words: "Are you sitting comfortably?"

◄ *US Airforce tour jacket, embroidered in Korea.*
£200–300

1952 1953 1954

- Death of George VI
- Eisenhower elected US President
- Identity cards abolished in Britian
- Britain tests her first atomic bomb, USA detonates H bomb
- Death of Eva Peron, wife of Argentinian Dictator
- Army coup in Egypt, King Farouk is exiled
- Mau Mau rebels create state of emergency in Kenya
- World's first jet airline service (London–Johannesburg)
- De Havilland 110 Jct fighter breaks the Sound Barrier
- Last trams run in London
- Contraceptive pill first manufactured
- Cinerama films first shown
- Olympic Games in Helsinki
- Invention of radio-carbon dating enables scientists to measure the age of ancient materials
- Agatha Christie's play *The Mousetrap*, begins its non-stop London run
- *New Musical Express* publishes the first British chart of best-selling singles

- Death of Stalin, Nikita Khrushchev becomes first secretary of the Communist Party
- Coronation of Elizabeth II, watched by 8,000 in Westminster Abbey and a television audience of around 25 million
- Edmund Hilary and Sherpa Tenzing conquer Everest
- Armistice ends fighting in Korea
- Military Coup in Iran overthrows Mossadeq and reinstates the Shah
- John F. Kennedy marries Jaqueline Bouvier
- Colour TV demonstrated in New York
- Christie hanged for a series of horrific murders at 10 Rillington Place
- Russians explode their H bomb
- Ian Fleming's *Casino Royale* introduces James Bond
- Hugh Hefner launches Playboy
- First car with fibreglass body, the Chevrolet Corvette
- Biologists James Watson and Francis Crick discover DNA molecule
- First tea bags marketed in Britain

- Dr Billy Graham crusades in the USA and Britain
- Fall of Senator McCarthy after condemation by US Senate
- Food rationing ends in Britain
- Nasser emerges as Egypt's Leader
- West Germany wins World Cup
- Roger Bannister runs the first mile in under four minutes
- Algerian Nationalists rise up against French rule
- Publication of *Lord of the Rings* by J.R.R. Tolkien, *Lord of the Flies* by W. Golding and *Lucky Jim* by K. Amis
- Nautilus launched as the world's first nuclear submarine
- Newspapers report recent discoveries of a link between smoking and cancer
- Audrey Hepburn wins an Oscar® for *Roman Holiday*
- Teddy boy hairstyles banned from British schools

▼ *The Coronation provided a welcome merchandising opportunity for toy manufacturers. This Coronation State Coach is boxed. £135–165*

► *First edition of William Golding's* Lord of the Flies (*Faber*). *£450–750 (without dust jacket £50–80)*

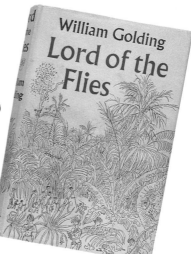

1955 1956 1957

- Winston Churchill retires
- Argentine Dictator Juan Peron is overthrown
- Ruth Ellis is the last woman to be executed in Britain
- Commercial Television begins in Britain, first TV advert promotes a toothpaste with a delicious tingle
- Wave of Flying saucer sightings
- First Wimpy opens in London
- American Supreme Court orders Southern schools to end segregation
- Fibre optics developed in Britain
- Opening of Disneyland in California
- British premiere of Samuel Becket's play *Waiting for Godot*
- Bill Haley releases *Rock Around the Clock*, James Dean stars in *Rebel Without a Cause* and dies in car crash

- Khrushchev denounces Stalin's reign of terror
- Hungarian uprising crushed by the Soviet forces; 20,000 people die, 200,000 flee to the West
- Egypt's President Nasser nationalizes Suez Canal precipitating the Suez Crisis
- Eisenhower returned as US President
- Transatlantic telephone service begins
- First video recorder manufactured
- First Eurovision song contest
- Real Madrid win first European Cup football competition
- Grace Kelly marries Prince Rainier of Monaco
- Marilyn Monroe marries Arthur Miller
- Premium bonds launched in Britain
- John Osborne's *Look Back in Anger* opens at London's Royal Court Theatre

- Harold Macmillan succeeds Eden as Prime Minister. He tells the electorate "You've never had it so good."
- Treaty of Rome establishes the European Economic Community
- Integration riots at Little Rock High School, Arkansas
- Russian Satellite Sputnik I circles the globe in 96 minutes, on Sputnik II Laika becomes the first dog in space
- American satellite Vanguard blows up
- Wolfenden Committee recommends the legalization of homosexual relations between consenting adults in private
- Deaths of Chistian Dior, Humphrey Bogart and Arturo Toscanini
- Sony market the first pocket-sized transistor radio
- Frisbees invented in the USA
- Queen announces that debutantes will no longer be presented at court
- First Parking meters in London

▼ *TV spawned a rash of related board games. Launched in 1955 and hosted by Hughie Green,* Double Your Money *was one of ITV's most popular shows. £15–20*

◀ *Space kitsch: cigarette dispenser and Sputnik ashtray by Bourne Terrace, London. £40–60*

1958 1959

- Setting up of the Campaign for Nuclear Disarmament (CND)
- China crushes national rising in Tibet; 65,000 Tibettans are killed and the Dalai Lama forced into exile
- Munich air disaster devastates Manchester United football team
- Brazil win soccer World Cup
- Race riots in Notting Hill, London
- John XXIII becomes Pope
- Launch of the *Carry On* film series
- Publication of *Dr Zhivago*
- Brussels Universal and International Exhibition
- Invention of the microchip
- Britain's first Top Ten LP Chart. The film soundtrack of *South Pacific* dominates no 1 spot for 1958 and all of 1959

- Vice President Nixon visits Moscow, debates with Khrushchev at the exhibition of an American dream kitchen
- Buddy Holly dies in plane crash
- NASA picks first Astronaut squad
- Hawaii becomes 50th US State
- Hovercraft makes maiden voyage
- First identikit pictures used for criminal identification
- Fidel Castro takes power in Cuba
- Conservatives increase majority in UK
- De Gaulle made President of France
- First Section of MI opened in Britain
- Unveiling of the Austin Mini
- Yves St Laurent predicts that skirts will rise above the knee

▼ *Centrepiece of Brussels 1958 Expo, was the Atomium, a 360 ft (110m) high model of an iron molecule, complete with restaurant. The stucture inspired many souvenirs including this 'build your own Atomium set". £50–100*

◄ *This is the US film poster for* Some Like it Hot *(1959), one of the greatest film comedies of the decade, directed by Billy Wilder and starring Jack Lemon, Tony Curtis and Marilyn Monroe as Sugar Kane (81x 41in [206 x 104cm]). £1400–1800*

Chronology

After

World War II

there was a pressing need

to house newly married couples,

families who had been bombed out and those

who were still living in slums. A survey in 1950 showed

that nearly half of all British homes had no bathroom. As towns

and apartments were built around the world, manufacturers catered for the

new, often smaller post-war home. Furniture became light and moveable: chairs stacked,

Homestyle

sofas folded out into beds, a trolley could be wheeled in for a TV dinner and converted into
an ironing board. The television became the focal point of the living room. Labour-saving
appliances replaced servants in the kitchen, where new materials such as vinyl and Formica
introduced easy-care surfaces and brilliant tones. After dull and drab wartime furnishings,
lust for colour and pattern expressed itself in every media, from mix-and-match tableware
to curtains emulating abstract paintings. Designers experimented with the latest technology
to create innovative forms: chairs floated on spidery metal legs, table tops were shaped like
amoebae, and lights looked like flying saucers. This section celebrates homestyle in the
1950s from the ultimate in designer elegance to the most exuberant chainstore kitsch.

American Seating

"Never before so much for so few", enthused *Life* magazine in 1954. The United States emerged from World War II as the richest and most powerful nation in the world and embarked upon a massive spending spree. As young couples moved into their new open-plan suburban homes, demand for furniture boomed. Technologies developed during the war were applied to the mass production of domestic goods: fibreglass used in the aircraft industry was transformed into gaily coloured chairs; nylon, invented in 1939 and employed for parachutes, revolutionized peacetime upholstery.

These new materials helped to create the New Look in furniture. Plastics and plywood could be moulded into organic and asymmetric shapes; slender and invariably splayed aluminium legs made the most substantial of seats appear to float in space. It was a golden age for American design. The leading furniture manufacturers such as Herman Miller and Knoll Associates recruited architects and sculptors, including George Nelson (1907–86), Harry Bertoia (1915–78), Eero Saarinen (1910–61) and, above all, Charles Eames (1907–78), who created a series of classic furniture designs for the 20th century.

► Known as the Butterfly, Sling or Hardoy, this was one of the favourite chairs of the 1950s. It was designed in 1938 by a group of Argentinian architects, among them Jorge Ferrari-Hardoy, and was inspired by a Victorian, military folding chair. Fitted to a tubular steel frame, the leather or canvas sling came in a variety of colours. This suede example was manufactured by Knoll, who tried and failed to obtain the copyright. The chair was produced in its millions by numerous 1950s manufacturers, cheap copies being advertised for under $15.

£150–250

◄ Designed by Eero Saarinen in 1946–8, this Womb chair and ottoman was made by Knoll. Its organic shape prefigured much 1950s design and was inspired by Florence Knoll's request for a chair large enough to curl up in. Saarinen saw the chair as "biological", designed to give physical and psychological comfort to modern sitters "who like to slouch". The mass production of the chair was made possible by new materials: a moulded fibreglass shell, foam rubber padding and tubular steel legs.

£1500–1800

► Paul Goldman (b.1912) designed for the American armed forces during World War II. This experience was to prove useful in peacetime manufacture. The Cherner chair was designed by Goldman in 1957 for his Plycraft company, based in Massachusetts, USA. Goldman exploited the properties of plywood to create a sculptural design, with extravagantly swept arms, elegant tapering legs, and a single moulded seat and back, with a slim-line waist. Feminine, and reflecting the hourglass lines of contemporary dress, this chair was formerly attributed to designer Norman Cherner.

£800–1100

▲ The Coconut chair was designed by George Nelson in 1956 for manufacture by Herman Miller. Nelson was one of the most influential post-war designers, credited with the concept of the shopping mall. As its name suggests, this fashionably capsule-shaped chair was modelled on a broken piece of coconut. For all its light-hearted appearance, the chair is heavy to move, thanks to its solid steel shell.

£1200–1800

◄ Sculptor Harry Bertoia claimed that his wire chairs were studies in space, form and the nature of metal. The Diamond chair with ottoman and the long-necked Bird chair came in both chrome-plated and plastic-coated wire. The latter is upholstered, a welcome addition since the "airy" exposed frame can be uncomfortable. One of Knoll's best-selling lines, Bertoia's chairs have remained in production since the early 1950s. Their royalties have allowed the designer to devote himself to a career in sculpture.

Diamond chair & ottoman **£200–300** *Bird chair* **£300–400**

17

▼ Working in partnership with his wife Ray (1913–88), Charles Eames was perhaps the most influential designer of the period. During World War II the couple used moulded plywood to produce leg splints for the United States Navy. This experimental wartime work helped shape their later furniture. Eames exhibited this wooden lounge chair in his one-man show at the Museum of Modern Art, New York, in 1946. "Eames has... produced the most important group of furniture ever developed in this country. His achievement is a compound of aesthetic brilliance and technical inventiveness", enthused *Arts & Architecture* magazine. The designs were revolutionary in technique: the complex curvature of moulded plywood, electric glueing, and the use of rubber shock mounts joining back and seat to wood and metal bases. Though these shock mounts enhanced the comfort of the chair by allowing some movement, since rubber is prone to perishing, extant examples can be damaged beyond repair. Good condition is crucial to the value of this classic chair made by Herman Miller. Designed for mass production, Eames' low cost, high-quality furniture is highly sought after today, and even his most utilitarian medical products such as the leg splints have been transformed into collectables.

£800–1000

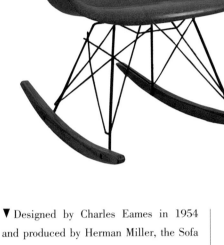

▼ Designed by Charles Eames in 1954 and produced by Herman Miller, the Sofa Compact was one of the first sofas to be flat-packed. The back folds down onto the seat and the legs are detachable; it was assembled by the customer. The slim-line geometric shape is typical of contemporary styling and reflects Eames' concern to create furniture that was practical from the moment it left the workshop.

£1700–2000

◄ Made from material developed for aircraft radar domes, the beauty of Eames' shell chair was that it was strong, cheap to produce and flexible. The variously moulded fibreglass shells came in a range of colours and were attached to different bases. These 1950s models, made by Zenith and Herman Miller, feature rocking chair and Eiffel Tower bases. Mainly purchased for offices, these chairs were also targeted at the housewife. Advertisements showed children sprawled all over these "lightweight beauties that never scuff or stain". The curved edges preserved its contours from damage and chairs are still likely to be found in good condition. Mass-produced for offices, these chairs were often dumped and are becoming harder to find today.

Rocking chair **£800–1000**
Green chair **£180–200** *Yellow chair* **£250–500**

► This leather lounge chair and ottoman, designed in 1956, was the last in Eames' series of plywood chairs and is probably his most famous and expensive creation. The model was conceived of as a chair in which Hollywood film director Billy Wilder could watch television. Masculine in style, the chair was the acme of luxurious and flexible comfort, with thick leather pads cradled in rosewood veneered shells, an articulated headrest (inspired by a barber's chair), and a swivel base. The chair was originally sold by Herman Miller for $634. Such is its popularity that it is still in production today although now that rosewood is a protected species, manufacturers use cherry veneer. Ironically, a contemporary version will cost around £2,500–3,000, twice as much as a period example.

£1200–1800

Scandinavian Seating

Furniture from Scandinavia, and in particular Denmark, was widely exported in the 1950s and became virtually synonymous with good taste. Danish Modern was the human face of the contemporary look, less alienating than the plastic excesses of avant-garde styling. Wood was the predominant material, much of it coming from the teak forests of Indo-China which had been felled to make way for roads. Inspired by functional classics such as the Windsor chair, craftsmen created furniture that was organic in feel, natural in colour and supremely practical. Items could be purchased singly rather than in suites. Light and simple designs were easy to transport and fitted comfortably into smaller post-war homes across the world. Danish furniture was not all bare wood and becoming modesty. Arne Jacobsen (1902–72) and Verner Panton (b.1926), experimenting with man-made materials, took furniture to new heights of technique and imagination. Their designs are hugely sought after today. Scandinavian furniture often appeals to the more academic enthusiast, with a love of fine craftsmanship and subtle restraint.

▲ Architect Finn Juhl (1912–89) became one of the famous exponents of the Danish Modern style. His influences included both the work of tribal craftsmen and contemporary artists, and he would often exhibit his furniture next to a piece of abstract sculpture in order to emphasize the close relationship between the two. This sofa was designed in 1946 and produced by cabinet maker Niels Vodder. Juhl has endowed a piece of stuffed furniture with a distinct sculptural presence – the curved silhouette gives a sense of movement to a traditionally earthbound and often clumsy furniture shape.

£850–1250

◄ Hans Wegner (b.1914) was one of Denmark's finest cabinet makers. He combined traditional craftmanship with an understanding of modern needs in order to create a series of functional classics. One 1949 seating design was so celebrated that it became simply known as The Chair. This beech, sawback armchair was designed for manufacturers Carl Hansen in 1951. The A-shaped legs were a favourite Wegner motif, their lines contrasting with the gentle curves of the upholstered seat and back.

£300–400

◄Designed by Hans Wegner, this lightweight, three-legged chair with beech frame and teak veneered seat was mass-produced by Fritz Hansen in the 1950s. In *Modern Danish Furniture* (1956) Esbjorn Hiort writes: "Greater simplification of form and structure is hardly possible in a chair made of wood, yet it is an expressive and individual piece of furniture. The fact that these chairs can be stacked one on top of the other is a great advantage.... Used at a round table, the three-legged structure assures the most economical utilization of space – an important consideration in a small flat."

£150–200

► This AX armchair designed in 1950 for Fritz Hansen by Peter Hvidt (b.1916) and Orla Molgaard Nielsen (b.1907) won the Diploma of Honour at the 1954 Milan Triennale. These two Danish architects formed a partnership after World War II to produce furniture specifically designed for export. Like a tennis racket, the AX chair was made from layers of laminated wood sandwiched and glued together and was light but strong. It was not only style and friendly wooden surfaces that made Danish furniture so successful but also pragmatic design. This chair could be transported flat-packed to be assembled in homes across the world.

£200–250

◄This two-seater sofa was designed by Prince Sigvard Bernadotte *c.*1954. Born in Sweden in 1907, Bernadotte also worked in many other media including silver and textiles. This sofa shows the 1950s fashion for ridding seating furniture of all-concealing upholstery. With its mahogany frame, slim padded seat and separate hinged adjustable backrests, this seat was one of the contemporary items featured on Enid Seeney's famous Homemaker plate (see p.59).

£500–600

"Steel tubes, foam, springs and covers have been so developed technically that we can create forms which were unthinkable just a few years ago. Designers should now use these materials to create objects which up to now they could only see in their dreams. Personally I'd like to design chairs which exhaust all the technical possibilities of the present." Verner Panton

◄ ▼ In the 1950s Arne Jacobsen was Denmark's leading architect working in the international modern style. His most celebrated commission was the Scandinavian Airlines System Royal Hotel and Air Terminal (1956–60) in Copenhagen for which he designed all the furniture and fittings including the Egg chair (left) and the Swan chair (below), illustrated here with matching sofa. Jacobsen used moulded fibreglass shells upholstered with foam rubber to create seating that was organic in shape and boldly abstract in appearance. Like Saarinen's Womb chair (see p.16), the Egg chair was designed to comfort and cradle the sitter. The Swan chair is based on the shape of a swan's wings; its form recalling Matisse cut-outs. Both designs were manufactured by Fritz Hansen, came in a variety of colours and materials and were retailed to the general public. These examples are covered in both fabric and vinyl. The foam padding used on much 1950s seating furniture is prone to crumbling, and period examples often need re-covering. Specialists recommend choosing a fabric with stretch properties and, above all, an upholsterer experienced in foam rubber.

Egg chair **£1500–2000** *Swan chair* **£400–600** *Swan sofa* **£1400–1800**

► The seat and legs of many 1950s chairs were treated as separate items and made from different materials. Verner Panton's interest lay in creating a chair in which they were unified into a single form. Produced in 1959, this Cone chair is constructed from folded sheet metal and upholstered with foam rubber. The dynamic design is enhanced by the swivel base and even today it looks futuristic. As Panton explains: "I concern myself above all with the material, the result then rarely has four legs, not because I do not wish to make such a chair, but because the processing of materials like wire or polyester calls for new shapes."

£350–500

◄ This extremely rare S-chair was designed by Verner Panton for Gebr. Thonet in 1954–55. Panton has folded a piece of laminated, white lacquered wood like a piece of chewing gum in his efforts to create a single form chair. Wood was not really the right material for such a liquid line: this chair is surprisingly heavy and has the feel of a piece of sculpture rather than furniture. However, Panton was a practical as well as imaginative designer, from this early work evolved the first, successful, one-piece plastic chair, designed in 1960. Technology caught up with Panton's imagination and chairs like this were mass-produced by Herman Miller in 1967. The orange version (above left) dates from the early 1970s.

Orange chair **£100–200** *White chair* **£1200–1600**

► Designed in 1952 this Ant chair was the most commercially successful of all Arne Jacobsen's designs. Made from moulded plywood, the back and seat were inspired by the shape of its animal namesake. It stands on spindly, insect-like metal legs and its hourglass form reflects the contemporary dress fashions. Light and stackable, the chair was mass-produced by Fritz Hansen in the 1950s and exported around the world. It is still in production today in a range of bright colours.

£100–150

Italian Seating

Italy emerged beaten and bruised after World War II. As in Britain, thousands of buildings had been destroyed, and there was an immediate need for housing and domestic goods. From this unpromising start emerged a renaissance in Italian design. Furniture makers began to employ leading architects to create modern furniture for mass production. Designers, including Marco Zanuso (b.1916) and Osvaldo Borsani (b.1911), experimented with new materials and sophisticated technology. Independent workshops produced exclusive and innovative furniture, ranging from the sculptural creations of architect Carlo Mollino (1905–73) to the graphic fantasies of artist Piero Fornasetti (1913–88). There was a huge variety in individual style but a unity in the overall aesthetic, with modern design and materials permeating every level of the market. Much of the furniture industry was centred in Milan, where the Milan Triennales offered an international showcase for new designers. Also, the Milan-based *Domus* magazine championed modern Italian design abroad. In this fertile and creative atmosphere the industry blossomed, and by the end of the decade Italy had become the world's leading exporter of modern furniture.

◄ In 1948 the Italian tyre company Pirelli commissioned architect Marco Zanuso to explore the possibilities of using foam rubber in furniture. His experiments resulted in the Lady armchair of 1951. Rather than being constructed with a traditional spring and horsehair filling, this wooden-framed chair used elastic webbing and foam rubber upholstery to create the feminine curved shape expressed in its name. The Lady chair won a gold medal at the 1951 Milan Triennale. It was produced by Arflex, the company established in 1950 to mass-produce these new designs. This example has been re-upholstered in black leather.

£1000–1400

▼ After the privations of war, there was a demand for colourful furniture. This Farthingale chair was designed by Marco Zanuso for Arflex in the 1950s. Standing on splayed legs with ball feet it is upholstered in foam rubber and covered with a brilliant blue fabric. A swathe of fabric on the back provides the skirted farthingale effect.

£1200–1600

► Made in Italy in the 1950s (makers unknown) these two ebonized side chairs reflect contemporary taste for linear, slender furniture. Architect Gio Ponti (1892–1979) pioneered this style with his celebrated Superleggera (super light) chair, a minimalist reinterpretation of a traditional rush-seated fisherman's chair, designed in 1956. A chair "must be light, slim and convenient", insisted Ponti. The ladderback chair (far right) conforms to Ponti's dictum and was inspired by traditional design but it has been updated by a tapering almost graphic black line. The elongated back of the other chair (right) recalls the silhouette of a church steeple, reflecting the Italian love of attenuated forms and flamboyant shapes.

£125–175 *Each*

"Superleggera"

◄Designed in 1954 by Italian architect Osvaldo Borsani (b.1911), the P40 chaise-longue was a machine-age version of Le Corbusier's famous reclining chair. A complex mechanism allows the chair to be adjusted into a remarkable 486 different positions. It can be transformed into an upright seat or even folded up altogether. The footrest is retractable and the rubber arms can be pushed downward. Condition is important with this technological masterpiece; over the years the cogs can seize up and limit its flexibility. The only design flaw is that the bendy arms make it difficult to get out of the chair. The P40 was manufactured by Borsani's company Tecno and is still in production today.

£1200–1500

"must be light, slim and convenient"

► This collection of *Domus* magazines dates from the 1950s. *Domus* was founded in 1928 by Gio Ponti who, with the exception of six years, was the editor until his death in 1979. It was a highly influential publication, championing Italian and other modern design around the world. Vintage issues are collected both as examples of period style and as research tools for identifying furniture and applied arts.

£8–10 *Each*

British Seating

Timber was in short supply in Britain post World War II. The Utility Scheme, launched to provide standardized basic and price-controlled furniture for those bombed out of their houses and for new homemakers, operated until the early 1950s. Even when restrictions were finally lifted, manufacturers remained conservative. "Still the same old stuff," complained Ernest Race in 1952, "bulky, ostentatious, over ornamented, and apparently polished by the process used for making toffee apples." Race (1913–64) was one of the few to experiment with modern design, and his skeletal metal chairs, created for the Festival of Britain (1951), became a spindly symbol of the new Elizabethan age. Robin Day (b.1915), another Festival contributor, was perhaps the most famous British designer of the period. Working for Hille Limited, he exploited new materials and pioneered the long, lean and simple architectural look that came to epitomize contemporary British style. "An appreciation of form stripped of vulgar excrescences", noted the *Daily Mail Ideal Home Book* in 1955. Day was among the winners of the first awards handed out by the Design Centre, opened in London in 1956. This showcase for British products became a fashionable venue, symbolizing the growing interest in contemporary design.

► This chair was designed by Robin Day in 1951 for the Royal Festival Hall, on London's South Bank, and was produced by Hille Limited. The curved back of the chair is formed from one piece of plywood; its padded back and seat is supported by a metal frame. The flared arms, useful for supporting drinks, were a distinctive Day hallmark. Radical in their time, Day's designs received a mixed response in the conservative press – "Is the whole thing a giant leg pull?" demanded the *Daily Sketch*.

£550–800

▼ Robin Day's convertible settee won a Design Centre award in 1957. Its design shows the move away from overstuffed upholstery and demand for dual-purpose furniture. This sofa-bed has been recovered with a reproduction of the original Mourne Check fabric, hand-woven by Gerd Hay-Edie, Day's textile designer. This faithful restoration reflects the respect now being paid to 1950s furniture.

£800–1000

► An Antelope chair and matching two-seater sofa designed by Ernest Race for the Festival of Britain in 1951. This seating was used both indoors and outdoors. The frames were made from stove-enamelled, rust-proofed steel rods; the seats from plywood, drilled with a line of holes for the drainage of rainwater. To prevent the spindly metal legs from piercing either the ground or people's toes, at first they were terminated by white ball feet, and then later by moulded plastic ferrules. The sofa is far rarer than the chair.

Chair **£60–120** *Sofa* **£400–600**

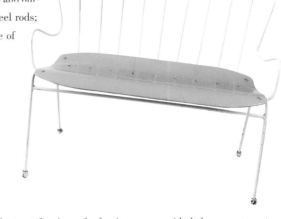

▼ Contract furniture for businesses provided the opportunity for designers to experiment with new techniques and materials suitable for mass-production. Commissioned by the shipping company P&O for their Orient line, this Neptune chair was produced by Ernest Race in 1953. The design was a modern version of a Victorian deck chair. The seat and back were moulded from pre-formed plywood and the legs were made from beech laminates. The chair was designed to stack easily and fold without the use of metal hinges, which would rust and corrode at sea.

£900–1200

► These beech and plywood Jason chairs were produced in 1950 by Danish architect Carl Jacobs for the London firm, Kandya Limited. The holes in the back of the chair were both decorative and practical as they allowed the chairs to be stacked easily and safely. The same low-cost design also came with metal legs and in a range of mix-and-match colours.

£250–400

Dining Furniture

The smaller size of the post-World War II home affected fashions in dining furniture. The kitchen was no longer hidden away "below stairs" but became a focal family room, often doubling up as a kitchen/diner. The American dinette is perhaps the ultimate example of furniture that was practical yet at the same time stylish enough for informal entertaining. Plastic surfaces tended to be restricted to the kitchen area, although Saarinen's pedestal furniture proved that chairs and tables could be "wipe clean" and still elegant enough for the smartest interior. When the dining room was separate or combined with the living room, more formal wooden furniture was favoured; "Scandinavian Modern" (or a look-alike equivalent) proved to be a favourite contemporary choice.

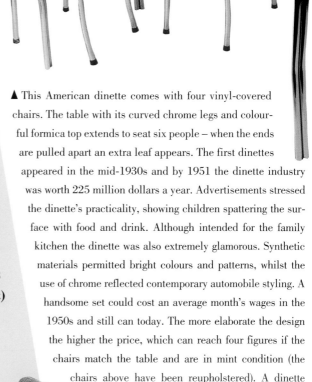

▲ This American dinette comes with four vinyl-covered chairs. The table with its curved chrome legs and colourful formica top extends to seat six people – when the ends are pulled apart an extra leaf appears. The first dinettes appeared in the mid-1930s and by 1951 the dinette industry was worth 225 million dollars a year. Advertisements stressed the dinette's practicality, showing children spattering the surface with food and drink. Although intended for the family kitchen the dinette was also extremely glamorous. Synthetic materials permitted bright colours and patterns, whilst the use of chrome reflected contemporary automobile styling. A handsome set could cost an average month's wages in the 1950s and still can today. The more elaborate the design the higher the price, which can reach four figures if the chairs match the table and are in mint condition (the chairs above have been reupholstered). A dinette with an integral mechanism is more desirable than one with a separate extension leaf.

Table & four chairs **£750–850**

◄ Compared to the American dinette, this English formica-topped kitchen table looks like a poor and ration-fed relation. Nevertheless, it is brightly coloured and unusual in that the set is in good condition and still includes its four matching chairs with their original upholstery.

Table & four chairs **£60–75**

"I wanted to make the chair all one thing again."

◄Eero Saarinen's Tulip chair and table (available in larger sizes) formed part of the pedestal furniture designed for Knoll in 1956. The American architect's aim was to create single form furniture. "The undercarriage of chairs and tables... makes an ugly, confusing, unrestful world. I wanted to clear up the slum of legs. I wanted to make the chair all one thing again", he explained. The chair is a fibreglass shell on an aluminium pedestal, coated white to create a continuous flowing whole. Although the effect was contemporary, Saarinen was unhappy with the compromise: "I look forward to the day when... the chair will be one material as designed." His disappointment did not prevent imitations, including copies by Arkana, which appear on the market more frequently than the Knoll originals.

Chair **£130–150** *Table* **£100–150**

►This pine and ebonized dining suite was produced by the Finnish designer Ilmari Tapiovaara (b.1914) for Asko in the late 1950s. The complete suite includes a table, two benches and four dining chairs. Finnish design came to prominence in the 1950s, gaining international acclaim at the Milan Triennales. Furniture was mass-produced and Asko was among the first companies to embrace contemporary design after World War II.

£700–1000

◄This ash table was designed by Italian architect Carlo Mollino (1905–73) for the Pavia restaurant in Cervinia *c.*1954. Mollino was one of the most respected and individualistic designers of the period. He produced a remarkable series of tables during the 1950s; the designs were both sculptural and organic, and always sensitive to the material used. The contents of the Pavia were dispersed at auction in the 1970s. Mollino's work is highly sought after. Although this table is rather wobbly its value remains high.

£4000–5000

29

Occasional Tables

For the average home owner in the 1950s it was easier and less expensive to create a contemporary look by buying a palette-shaped coffee table than by investing in a three-piece suite. Large furniture required a major commitment in terms of money, space and taste. With a small occasional table, cheap to buy and easy to dispose of when fashions changed, everyone could afford a piece of the New Look. Innovative, one-off creations by the leading designers of the day filtered down into factory-made, low-cost furniture. Occasional tables came in a multiplicity of styles reflecting the fashion for organic and dynamic shapes and colourful patterns. Since so many different examples were manufactured (coffee, side and telephone tables), a wide range of tables is still readily available today, and prices remain fairly reasonable.

► The kidney-shaped coffee table became one of the design clichés of the period. It was both fashionable and practical, the curved line fitting snugly around the arm of a chair or sofa. Various interpretations have been offered for the popularity of the amoeboid form in 1950s design. These range from the influence of modern art to the effect of scientific developments, from the wings of a jet plane to camouflage patterns during World War II. Whatever its origins, certainly after the harsh austerity of war and the lean lines of utility fashions, the public were hungry for rounded forms and fun designs, and the kidney shape was adopted for everything from coffee tables to swimming pools. The Zambezi coffee set is by Midwinter (see British Ceramics, p.56). **£10–15**

◄ The palette was a favourite 1950s motif, used in jewellery, ceramics, textiles and across different media. Many designs were influenced by contemporary art and this table takes artistic inspiration at its most literal. The vinyl "wood-look" top is supported on metal legs. Three-legged furniture was a popular feature and the tops and legs of tables, as with chairs, were often made from different materials. Like the kidney-shaped table, variations on this design were mass-produced by different manufacturers. **£20–25**

►In the 1940s and 1950s ballet was one of the most popular art forms. Margot Fonteyn was the idol of a generation, many of whom tuned in to the BBC's "Ballet for Beginners", one of the most popular programmes on television. Ballerinas decorated everything from head scarves to china or, as here, a coffee table. The reproduced image is protected by a glass top and the table stands on tapered wooden legs. Similar tables came decorated with various designs ranging from abstract patterns to Venetian canals. Price depends on the appeal of the image.

£20–30

"Balletomania was rampant." Bevis Hillier

◄The 1950s saw many artists becoming involved with the decorative arts. With artist Nigel Henderson, British sculptor Eduardo Paolozzi (b.1924) founded the company Hammer Prints to produce and market designs for ceramics, textiles and wallpapers. This metal-framed table dates from *c.*1956 and was designed by Henderson with ceramic tiles by Paolozzi.

£600–800

"takes wear like a rhino's hide"

►As the television inspired comfortable television armchairs, so this table, made in the United States in the 1950s, was designed for the telephone. "English people never know what it is. The telephone table is a typically American innovation", claims the owner. The heavy wooden base reflects the fashion for asymmetric styling, the table top is covered in formica and the seat in vinyl. Vinyl upholstery became increasingly popular on American furniture, providing a cheap lookalike alternative to more luxurious leather, and a durable stain-resistant surface. "As tender to touch as a baby's skin, but takes wear like a rhino's hide", boasted a leading manufacturer of synthetic textiles. The lamp, too, is American.

£100–150

Storage Furniture

Like the open-plan room, built-in storage furniture was a distinguishing feature of the 1950s home. Wardrobes were replaced by fitted cupboards; individual cabinets gave way to multipurpose shelves and units, which also served as room dividers, splitting an open interior into living and dining areas. Traditional sideboards remained popular in Britain, but adopted long and boxy shapes: "static and architectural, contrasting with free and sprightly looking chairs and tables which are obviously mobile and three-dimensional", explained British designer Robin Day in 1957. Built-in furniture, especially the introduction of the fitted kitchen, fulfilled many practical requirements, but some storage needs were resolved with more whimsical solutions. The fashion for cocktail cabinets inspired many extravagant designs, while lust for decoration created items designed uniquely for the display of ornaments or plants. One of the most archetypal storage pieces of the period was also one of the smallest: the magazine rack, which became a standard feature in almost every living room.

▲ This photograph was used as an advertisement in 1957 by E. Gomme Limited, makers of G-Plan furniture. Founded in 1925, Gomme created designs that were moderate in price and modern in idiom. Individual pieces of G-Plan furniture can still be picked up for very little cost and could well prove to be a good investment. A complete room divider, as shown here, is far rarer and correspondingly more expensive.

£200–400

▼ This birch-veneered sideboard was designed by Robert Heritage (b.1927) for the English firm G. W. Evans and Company in 1954. The door panels were illustrated by Dorothy Heritage, the silk-screen design showing the decorative influence of Fornasetti. The box-like shape floating on slim tapered supports was typical of the period. "It may be that legs are on the way out", mused the *Studio Year Book 1959–60*, "chests, cupboards, storage units are poised on little legs, tiny ballbearing ankles... Perhaps the thought of flight, in space and outer space, compels the imagination of the designer...".

£1300–1800

◀ It was not only kitchen tables that were given brightly coloured plastic surfaces. This wooden sideboard unit is covered in red padded vinyl. The surfaces are black formica and the sliding doors striped glass. Even though the exterior of this British-made cabinet might boast modern materials and a "gay" fashion colour, inside it still contains a traditional green baize drawer for storing cutlery.

£80–120

▼ The *Studio Year Book 1958–59* noted the move toward combining plastic surfaces with wooden furniture: "these are being successfully applied to table tops and they make very effective facings for sideboards". This rosewood cocktail cabinet stands on square metal supports. The plastic laminated doors and reverse panel are decorated with cocktail glasses and bottles, the long-necked vessels and linear graphics reflecting the influence of Italian design.

£500–700

▲ This American tallboy (double chest of drawers) forms part of a 1950s bedroom suite, which also includes a matching bed, two bedside tables, a mirror and a dressing table. Made from an extremely heavy and solid oak base, the surface is covered with plasticized veneer. Artificial shading emphasizes the lines of the design and gives the wood-look laminate its own plastic patina. Not every manufacturer was producing modern designs, and there was still demand for traditional pieces of furniture, albeit exploiting the benefits of modern materials. The design of this tallboy reflects the lingering influence of Art Deco, which manifests itself in various forms in the 1950s, for example in the shape of early television cabinets.

— *Bedroom suite* **£1200–1500**

▶The fashion for cocktails in the 1950s inspired some playful designs, sometimes verging on the surreal. Bars came in a wide variety of shapes and styles. The boat cocktail bar was a popular conceit. Made from moulded plywood the base or "hull" is covered with plastic, simulated wood laminate, its tiny brass legs enhancing the "floating" effect. The glass and formica "deck" top contains an integral light, and the nautical styling extends to providing portholes, a rope railing and even a brass anchor. Boat bars like this were mass-produced by the English company Barget and appear on the market comparatively frequently.

£100–130

◀Belonging to a self-confessed addict of glamorous kitsch, this cocktail bar epitomizes the fun side of 1950s style. Still in daily use, it is shown *in situ* complete with period decorated glasses and a wealth of cocktail equipment (fake tiger-skin ice bucket, pin-up doll Martini shaker), reflecting the extravagant and often risqué motifs popular in objects associated with drinking and smoking. This exotic cocktail bar is made from bamboo; its top is covered with black formica inset with golden glitter. The bar stools are bamboo and cane, with elegant and elongated splayed metal legs.

Bar **£350–450**   *Bar stools* **£40–60**

◄ Curious, asymmetric shelving units were a popular feature of the period, often combined with a table and designed for the display of "knick-knacks" and plants. Made in Germany, this example is almost an exercise in how many different materials can be squeezed into a single piece of furniture, as it includes several kinds of wood, various formica surfaces, a brass trim and a wrought iron hoop topped off with a fetching design in plastic string.

£440–550

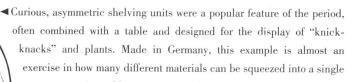

"There is no boundary between a craftwork and a work of art. It is all art." Piero Fornasetti (1913–88)

► The Italian designer Fornasetti was extremely prolific during the 1950s (see p.24). No object was too humble to receive the distinctive Fornasetti treatment. Umbrella stands, wastepaper baskets or, as here, an enamelled wooden magazine rack were beautifully decorated with an eclectic range of images drawing on both contemporary life and history. He is perhaps the only artist whose designs for such items can now be expected to fetch very high prices at auction.

£75–95

◄▼ The expansion of the magazine market in the 1950s spawned a matching growth in the production of magazine racks. For those who could not afford a Fornasetti original, there were plenty of alternatives. This selection includes a plywood example painted with a red and white abstract pattern, a folding magazine rack wrapped in black and white plastic, and models in wirework (a favourite 1950s medium) both standing on brightly coloured "cocktail cherry" feet. Magazine racks were produced in their thousands and are still readily found and reasonably priced today.

£8–15

Lighting

"Today we are at the beginning of an exciting new era," enthused the *Daily Mail Ideal Home Book* in 1957, "the development of what are from the historical viewpoint absolutely brand new lighting methods." The 1950s was a golden age in lighting. Inspired by contemporary art, Italian designers transformed lamps into domestic sculpture, providing elegant and sophisticated solutions to practical problems. Scandinavia, unsurprisingly given the nature of its climate, was another leader in the lighting field, while in the United States, George Nelson's "bubble" lamp and the paper globe lanterns produced by Isamu Noguchi (1904–88) provided archetypal shapes that are still in use today.

Variety in design was limitless – lamps came with adjustable length drops, twisting arms and mix-and-match coloured shades. "There is so much to choose from," claimed the *Daily Mail Ideal Home Book* in 1956, "the coolie hat, the 1920s cloche hat, the flying saucer, and many, many others. The materials are well varied too: plastic, raffia, paper, aluminium to mention but a few." Quality was equally diverse, ranging from the most stylish creations by the leading international designers to the ultimate in cheerful mass-produced kitsch. Each sought to make the interiors of 1950s homes more interesting, and both designer and kitsch lighting have their modern day collectors.

◀This Artichoke hanging lamp was designed in 1958 by the Danish architect Poul Henningsen (1894–1967) for the Langeline Pavilion Restaurant, Copenhagen. The Artichoke lamp is a contemporary version of the chandelier; crystal drops are replaced by overlapping steel leaves, which both reflect the light and diffuse the glare. Manufactured by Louis Poulsen, the lamp was also adapted for the domestic market, its decorative and surprising form illuminating interiors across the world.

£800–1200

▼ Plastics changed the shape of lighting as well as furniture. The Bubble lampshade was created by American designer George Nelson for Howard Miller in 1952; this classic design has inspired countless globular imitations. The shade was formed from a wire skeleton sprayed with vinyl coating to create a tight, translucent skin. Unfortunately, given the tendency of plastic to discolour with age and heat, this skin could end up looking a little jaundiced and lighting manufacturers had to be careful to use heat resistant plastics.

£150–200

▼ In 1932 Marcel Duchamp coined the word "mobile" to explain Alexander Calder's hanging sculptures, which the artist himself described as "my moving Mondrians". The designs of Calder and the colours of Mondrian had considerable influence on 1950s design, particularly in lighting, as reflected in this handsome

"my moving Mondrians"

ceiling lamp (maker unknown). Sculptural in effect, the lamp is composed of a brass rod with three circular uplighter shades springing like flowers from a stem.

£650–850

► Italian designers produced many elegant standard lamps in the 1950s. This example is brass, with articulated branches and spun aluminium multi-coloured shades. The hourglass shape was popular during the period and reflected the New Look in fashion, with its cinched waist and full skirt. Many lampshades mirror the design of contemporary hats and, according to one collector, the best continental lighting often has something of the slim and stylish elegance of Audrey Hepburn.

£350–500

◄ Italian brothers Achille (b.1918) and Pier Giacomo (1913–68) Castiglioni created some of the most innovative lighting produced this century. The Luminator was designed in 1954 and still looks astonishingly modern today. Manufactured by Gilardi Arform, the slim metal tube on slender tripod legs stands some 69in (175cm) high (excluding the bulb). The brothers took the linear, graphic style that permeates much of Italian design to its minimalist conclusion. Using industrial materials, they created rational and stylish solutions for new technologies. The reproduction light shown here cost a great deal less than an original example from the period.

Reproduction **£99** *Original* **£200–300**

►In the 1950s wall lights were a commonplace fixture in many living rooms. "Designed for permanent siting, they can be selected in the first place to give the required amount of light... and secondly, to fit either unobtrusively or as decorative motifs into the surrounding detail", advised the *Studio Year Book 1957–58*. The double-branch wall light featured here has glass shades and an amoeba-like base. There were many variations on this design that slipped comfortably into innumerable British homes during the period.

£24–28

▼ Fascination with space-age shapes influenced many designs in the decade that witnessed the launch of Sputnik and the start of the space race. These desk lamps resemble flying saucers. Both are on angular brass stems with metal shades. The black lamp was designed by Louis Kalft for the Dutch company Philips in 1959; the white model is French and was created in 1952 by Pierre Guariche for Disderot.

White lamp **£250–350** *Black lamp* **£120–180**

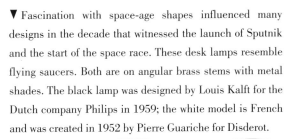

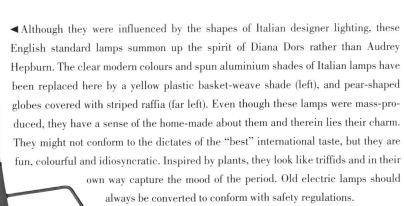

◄Although they were influenced by the shapes of Italian designer lighting, these English standard lamps summon up the spirit of Diana Dors rather than Audrey Hepburn. The clear modern colours and spun aluminium shades of Italian lamps have been replaced here by a yellow plastic basket-weave shade (left), and pear-shaped globes covered with striped raffia (far left). Even though these lamps were mass-produced, they have a sense of the home-made about them and therein lies their charm. They might not conform to the dictates of the "best" international taste, but they are fun, colourful and idiosyncratic. Inspired by plants, they look like triffids and in their own way capture the mood of the period. Old electric lamps should always be converted to conform with safety regulations.

Tripartite lamp **£100–130** *Single lamp* **£50–60**

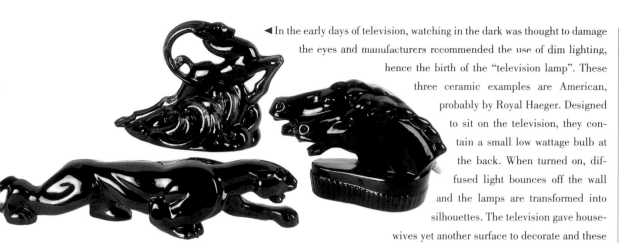

◄ In the early days of television, watching in the dark was thought to damage the eyes and manufacturers recommended the use of dim lighting, hence the birth of the "television lamp". These three ceramic examples are American, probably by Royal Haeger. Designed to sit on the television, they contain a small low wattage bulb at the back. When turned on, diffused light bounces off the wall and the lamps are transformed into silhouettes. The television gave housewives yet another surface to decorate and these lamps reflect the lingering influence of Art Deco design. Animal shapes were a popular choice, particularly the streamlined panther, symbolic of speed. In 1950 Royal Haeger advertised china black panther ornaments for as little as $1.50. In the current market the lamp versions of this design are worth considerably more. Other popular designs include galleons and figures.

£100–130 *Each*

► The fashion for this type of figurative lamp developed in the United States in the 1940s and 1950s. Bases are made in plaster and inspired by exotic prototypes such as Nubian slaves and Spanish dancers – shapes that allowed for lively movement and, in the case of female examples, scanty clothing. Often coming in male and female pairs, these lamps can be huge, sometimes weighing as much as 10–15lb (4.5–6.8kg). The parchment, two-tier shade on the matador light (far right) measures an arm span in diameter. Shades are collectable in their own right. The Venetian shade shown here (right) was a popular design; light streams up in slices through the metal slats and pours down below. highlighting the exuberant stand.

Nubian **£100–130** *Matador* **£200–250**

Technology

The 1950s saw radical developments that were to change the layout of the home and the life of its inhabitants. By 1954 nine out of ten American families owned a television, while in Britain the number of sets jumped from 14,560 in 1947 to 4,503,766 in 1955, the year that saw the launch of Independent Television. Television supplanted the fireplace as the focal point of the living room. It influenced room design, leisure activities and eating habits, as families snacked in front of the television set. Radio manufacturers fought back with new designs and marketing strategies. The invention of the transistor in 1948 led to the development of the pocket-sized transistor radio, launched by Sony in 1957. Plastic enabled affordable sets to be produced in a variety of different "fashion" shapes and colours, and radios were targeted at new audiences such as children and teenagers. The emergence of the youth market with money to spend and their own music to listen to affected manufacture in many areas, and demand for portable record players was fuelled by rock and roll.

Even that most traditional form of technology, the clock, was affected by new styles and developments. Conceived at the dawn of the 1950s, George Nelson's Ball clock became one of the most influential designs of the decade, a visible symbol of the new atomic age.

▲ This Bush 22 television was made in 1950. The influence of Art Deco is visible in the use of Bakelite and geometric styling. The 1950s price was £35 10s, the equivalent of more than a month's average wages. Television was given a huge boost by the coverage of the Coronation of Queen Elizabeth in 1953, attracting some 25 million people. Houses of those with televisions were packed with neighbours and friends, many of whom then bought or rented their own sets.

£150–200

◀ The portable television set was introduced in the United States in 1955. It created an even greater demand for televisions by encouraging families to purchase a second set, or even a set for every family member. Emphasizing the television's mobility, this advertisement shows the set being carried in one hand. In reality however, the sets were heavy and cumbersome and their portability was limited.

£150–250

◄ This Wegavision 2000 television has a cream plastic case and reflects the development in the late 1950s of the swivel screen, which allowed viewing from any angle in the room. The most celebrated example was the Predicta, manufactured in 1958 by Philco Corporation in the United States. They refined the design still further by creating a screen that not only turned, but could be detached from its base and moved around the house, thanks to a 25ft (7.6m) cable. The ultimate in fashionable mobility, this design was not very convenient given the length of cord and the fact that the television controls remained with the console. Philco claimed credit for the invention of the swivel set, although in fact their idea had already been anticipated by European manufacturers. The fashion for this twisting television did not last long and it was soon superseded by new and smaller portable sets.

£150–200

► The Bush TR2 portable transistor radio was produced by Bush Radio Limited, Plymouth, c.1959. This model, 12in (30cm) wide with a robust plastic case, exemplifies the flexibility of the transistor radio. It was promoted as a practical indoor/outdoor radio, coming complete with "handbag" carrying strap and a socket for car aerial. The large tuning dial, with its chrome knob and trim, was easy to use.

£10–12

◄▼ Manufactured in the United States, these Crosley radios date from the 1950s. Their design was inspired by the car dashboard, with large and impressive chrome dials and colourful plastic cases, and reflects the attempt by manufacturers to turn radios into fun, disposable items, targeted at young consumers. Radios from the 1950s are very popular in the current market, and the more extravagant their appearance, the higher the price. Collectors are also attracted by the warm, rich sound of valve radios. Values are determined by colour, condition and, above all, a distinctive style.

£175–275

▲ The American 500 phone (left) was designed in 1950 for the Bell Telephone Company by Henry Dreyfus (1904–72). More common in black than grey, it has a distinctive bell-like ring, familiar from 1950s B-movies. Far more radical was the Swedish Ericofon, also known, thanks to its upright design, as the Cobra phone. This was the world's first one piece telephone, produced in 1954 by L. M. Ericsson. The dial and circuitry were lodged in the base, and the design came in various colours.

Bell telephone **£25–45** *Ericofon* **£65–75**

► Made for the German company Braun, this radiogram was designed in 1956 by Dieter Rams (b.1932) and Hans Gugelot (1920–65). The design is known as Snow White's Coffin, owing to its rectangular, boxy shape and the transparent Plexiglas cover, which has become a standard feature of record player styling.

£225–300

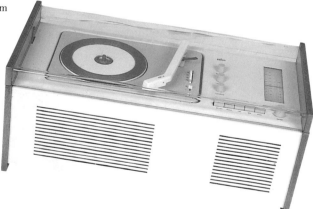

◄ This portable record player represents the antithesis of Braun's rationalist principles. Disguised as a handbag, the tiny and ladylike gramophone is contained in a heart-shaped Antler vanity case, covered with leopard-skin vinyl and lined with quilted pink satin. This fanciful confection shows how record players, like other equipment, were targeted at a younger, fashion-conscious market in the 1950s. In electrical appliances, as in dress, animal skin was a popular motif. Radios were decorated with snakeskin, and in 1959 Roberts unveiled a transistor radio covered in real mink which retailed at £156.

£150–250

► This Atom or Ball wall clock was created by George Nelson for American manufacturers Howard Miller in 1949. A design classic, it spawned countless imitators in the 1950s and inaugurated the fashion for "atomic" furnishings, with the use of metal supports and brightly coloured ball feet (also known as the "cocktail cherry" style). The clock is made from brass, steel and wood. Like many designs in the 1950s, it was inspired by scientific and space-age imagery, reflecting the shape of a star and the patterns of atomic and molecular structure.

£400–450

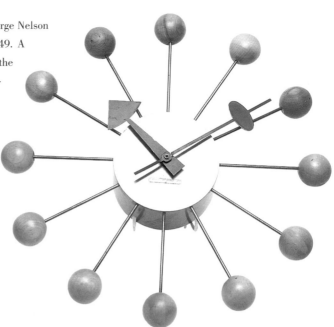

◄ If science and nuclear physics constituted one major design influence in the 1950s, Surrealism represented another. Made in England, and produced by Metamec Electric, this bright orange alarm clock is shaped like a staring, sleepless eye, a favourite surreal motif and a suitable image for an object designed to wake one up. The shiny spokes radiating from the centre or pupil recall the star shape of Nelson's influential Atom design, and the clock comes complete with an integral bedside light.

£20–30

► This Teasmade was created by Brenner Thornton for the British firm Goblin. Although it first retailed in 1937, sales were interrupted by the war and did not take off until the 1950s, when the Goblin Teasmade became a familiar domestic item and a favourite gift. The company benefited from free publicity, since the Teasmade often featured as a prize on the new television game shows. Initially called the "Cheerywake", it was designed to make the tea before waking you up. Water boiled in the kettle and poured through a pipe into the earthenware teapot. The weight of the tea activated the light, setting off the alarm. The Teasmade came complete with two cups and saucers, milk jug and sugar basin. This example is in perfect working order and includes the original melamine tray, which was often discarded over the years.

£30–36

Kitchen Appliances

After World War II, with the disappearance of servants for all but the most wealthy, the housewife moved into the kitchen. Because units and equipment were being used daily, quality and styling were transformed. The 1950s saw the development of the fitted kitchen and, since the room often doubled as a dining or living area, colour and cheerfulness were introduced into a previously all-white zone. Easy-care plastic and vinyl brightened up everything from floor tiles to table tops; curtains, decorated with pictures of food and drink, celebrated the end of austerity. Human help was replaced by labour-saving appliances and the United States pioneered the technology and the potent marketing concept of the "dream kitchen". With the growing interest in industrial design, many objects created for the 1950s kitchen have found their way into antique shops. Some command high prices, particularly American-influenced products, with their space-age shapes and confident glamour. Other domestic equipment can often be picked up from junk shops for less than their original 1950s prices. Optimistic enthusiasts maintain that with a little care these vintage machines can match the performance of their modern descendants while fulfilling their functional role with more style.

◀ In this publicity still from the 1950s a housewife proudly shows off her new cooker. Men might have held the purse strings but it was women who chose the household goods and whom manufacturers specifically targeted. Rarely are women in advertisements shown working. Typically they wear stilettos and party dresses, so overcome by the wonder of their new appliances that all they can do is grin and point. Social historians have argued that rather than liberating women from domestic chores, these "labour-saving" devices created more housework and higher domestic standards, isolating the housewife in her machine-filled home.

£30–50

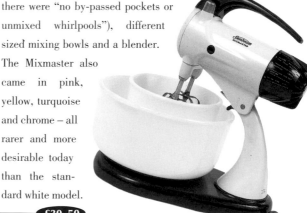

▼ Dating from the 1950s, this Sunbeam Mixmaster was one of the most popular food mixers on the American and British markets. The swivelling tailfin was inscribed with precise settings for every function from mixing muffins and quick breads to "lower speed less pulp juicing". The mixer could be detached from its stand for hand use, and attachments included "bowl fit" beaters (making sure there were "no by-passed pockets or unmixed whirlpools"), different sized mixing bowls and a blender. The Mixmaster also came in pink, yellow, turquoise and chrome – all rarer and more desirable today than the standard white model.

£30–50

◀This turquoise-blue "Juice 'O' Mat – Tilt Top Juicer" (left) was manufactured by Rival MFG Company, Kansas City, USA, c.1955. Like many American appliances it mirrors contemporary automobile design with the use of bright colour, gleaming chrome and a large, dynamic shape. Space imagery was another important decorative influence. Made in Austria c.1957, this Pinguin ice crusher (far left) is styled like a rocket. The translucent red plastic ice catcher makes this model particularly desirable and it is also rare to find ice crushers with stands, since they were generally wall mounted. The chrome British-made waffle maker (below left) produced by SLR Electric Limited reflects the shape of a flying saucer. A similar model was shown in the *Daily Mail Ideal Home Exhibition Book 1950–51*, the caption drawing particular attention to the lid with "its specially designed hinge which allows it to rise during cooking and so produce a waffle of even thickness."

Juicer **£65–75** *Ice crusher* **£80–100** *Waffle maker* **£60–80**

"Big and beautiful"

▶In 1939 only 200,000 British homes had refrigerators, but by 1959 annual sales had reached 750,000 as the refrigerator gradually progressed from being a luxury to a standard item in the post-war kitchen. As well as classic white models, manufacturers, particularly in the United States, produced coloured refrigerators, largely in the hope of increasing sales by turning the refrigerator into a "fashion" item that could be discarded and replaced like last season's dress. This British model was made by the General Electric Company (GEC). "Big and beautiful," boasted a 1955 advertisement, "here indeed is luxury living. A refrigerator styled with modern elegance, spacious enough to store an abundance of every kind of food and beverage you need for modern entertainment." The capacity of these refrigerators can seem comparatively small given their large bulbous casings. Nevertheless they are much sought after and, according to their owners, very reliable.

£350–400

"Washday drudgery is gone forever"

►The washing machine was one of the most coveted and costly of all domestic items. "Washday drudgery is gone for ever; More time for yourself; No more rough, red hands; More energy left for pleasure", promised the advertisers. Housewives were seduced by the idea of doing something else, while the laundry did itself. However, until the end of the decade and the introduction of hire purchase, only the comparatively well off could afford a washing machine. Dating from the late 1950s, this Servis Supertwin Mark II twintub was the ultimate in luxury, combining washer and spin dryer in a single cabinet, as opposed to having two machines or washer topped with a hand operated mangle. Using powder detergent, which required less hot water than soap, the twin tub was praised for its ability to cope with delicate and man-made fibres.

£50–100

"Brighter!" "Whiter!"

◄These 1950s washing powder and starch packets are all unopened and still contain their original contents. Most domestic goods were sold pre-packed post-World War II, and the design of the boxes and wrappers was all important. Packaging was produced in strong colours to attract the housewife and simplified designs emphasized the name of the brand. Soap manufacturers advertised heavily in woman's magazines, each one promising a "Brighter! Whiter! Washday" than it's rivals.

£4–8

► Produced in France in the early 1950s, this meta-morphic trolley converts into an ironing board. With its fashionable colours and space saving design, it epitomizes 1950s domestic requirements when, partly thanks to television, mobile furniture became popular.

£200–300

▼ The Hotpoint Company gained its name from producing an iron which radiated as much heat from its point as from its centre. With its stream-lined shape and curved black Bakelite handle, this Hotpoint iron exemplifies 1950s ergonomics. Even irons were prone to fashionable styling. "How thrilled you'll be with an HMV super all-purpose iron", promised an advertisement offering an HMV iron "in four gay colours". As its owner candidly admits, this iron is probably more interest-ing than valuable and were it not in pristine condition, it would be virtually worthless.

£15–20

◄ With its planet shape and space-age name, the Hoover Constellation designed in 1955 was the epitome of stylish, domestic technol-ogy. "Through its unique air lift, the new Constellation glides after you under its own air power", explained the publicity. It has a swivelling spherical top, and a hose that stretches to clean inaccessible areas. The Constellation featured in Richard Hamilton's 1956 collage *Just what is it that makes today's homes so different, so appeal-ing?*, a witty celebration of consumerism and one of the first Pop Art pictures. This particular model is in immaculate condition.

£60–80

▲ Advertisements from the period show women wearing insubstantial, aprons – designed so that the housewife could greet her guests without concealing her dress. Many aprons were produced in gaily printed cottons, matching table-cloths and kitchen curtains. Cotton aprons can be picked up for very little cost. This American apron is a little more sophisticated, presum-ably intended for cocktail hour.

£10–15

47

Food and Drink

The end of World War II did not bring an end to food rationing, which lasted in Britain until 1954. The welcome return of eggs, sugar and fats inspired a huge upsurge of interest in baking. Housewives striving to make the perfect sponge cake were aided by an expanding choice of equipment, ranging from expensive electrical appliances to inexpensive plastic kitchenware: easy to clean, hard to break and above all colourful. After the austerity of wartime food, people wanted fun. Cookbooks revelled in decorative presentation, showing how to sculpt tomatoes into flowers and smother puddings with piped cream and glacé cherries. Rationing had made it hard to invite people for a meal, and the 1950s saw the fashion for more spontaneous entertaining and informal everyday eating habits. "Television meals are the established routine in many homes... eaten not at a table but from a tray upon the knees", observed a 1957 advertisement for tinned vegetables. Television both advertised and inspired instant culinary gratification. In 1953 Swanson's introduced America to the first frozen "TV Dinner" – turkey, whipped sweet potatoes and garden peas – "old -fashioned goodness ready to eat in 25 minutes". Following the American lead, frozen and convenience foods became increasingly popular in Britain, sold in disposable packets, purchased from new self-service stores that sprang up during the decade, and consumed in front of the television.

▲ The Scandinavians provided classic designs for the kitchen as well as for furniture. This handsome black and white saucepan with its curved handle was made in Norway and reflects contemporary demand for kitchenware that was stylish enough to use in the oven and on the dining table.

£25–30

▲ These two wooden bowls and matching tray were designed by Jens H. Quistgaard for the Danish firm, Dansk Design. Made from solid teak, these examples are large and heavy (the tray and longer bowl are *c.*23½in [60cm] long). Dansk's simple, elegant products were exported across the world. In 1958 the tray was featured in the *Studio Year Book*, the annual furnishing bible for the stylish home-owner.

Set **£200–250**

◄ Red and white were very popular colours for kitchenware during the period, and this set of American canisters was retailed under the name of Gay Ware. Gay (in its original sense) was a favourite 1950s word, endlessly used in advertisements and trade names. The traditional four canister group (flour, sugar, coffee, tea) has been expanded to include a whole range of different containers. It is rare to find such a complete set, and when not in use, the canisters can be fitted into each other like Russian dolls.

£30–40

► Made in Japan by Woodpecker Woodware, this "Doggie Snack Server" is not the kind of object that would have featured in the *Studio Year Book*. Nevertheless, it does reflect the 1950s fashion for more relaxed and informal entertaining, with buffet suppers and finger food. "Dips are becoming very popular," noted Nella Whitfield in *Fun With Food* (1959), "tasty mixtures into which... small portions of food on cocktail sticks can be 'dunked'."

£8–10

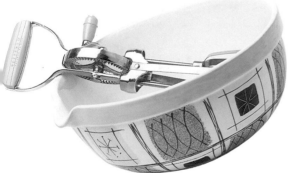

◄ This unusual mixing bowl was produced by Price Kensington, its colours and fashionably abstract pattern recalling contemporary designs in textiles. The same company also made a matching measuring jug and rolling pin. The rotary whisk with plastic handle and stainless steel beaters was produced by Prestige. Its solidly designed mechanism still functions perfectly today.

Bowl **£16–22** *Whisk* **£8–10**

► Reflecting the fashion for fun with food and decorative presentation, British manufacturers Nutbrown produced novelty party biscuit cutters that could transform biscuits and sandwiches into a whole range of fanciful shapes. The colourful packaging adds to the interest of this original 1950s set, as does the fact that it is complete. It contains a man in the moon, a star and a flower. When buying boxed sets, check that the contents are still intact. Another British manufacturer, Tala, made similar products.

£10–14

▶The fashion for cocktails inspired some of the most bizarre decorative extravagances of the period (see also Fabulous Kitsch on pp.74–5). Stereotyped images of black people were a favourite theme. The understandably miserable-looking native tribesman (far right) is ceramic and contains a range of cocktail accessories. He is clasping a small spoon instead of a spear. Marked "Lisa Valtiery" and made in Germany, the lady in the Carmen Miranda hat (right) is a decorative bottle top, her colourful skirt concealing not a pair of shapely legs but a cork. Tastes and social mores have changed since the 1950s and today some of these whimsical creations can appear frankly dubious. Nevertheless, particularly in the United States, there is a growing demand for so-called "black" memorabilia, notably among black collectors. Like pin-up material, such objects reflect the kitsch side of 1950s style.

Left **£20–25** *Right* **£25–30**

"a delicious, exhilarating drink"

◀The rise of the Italian coffee bar in 1950s Britain did much to promote the popularity of coffee as a drink for young people. The first coffee bar was opened in Soho in the early 1950s, and by the end of the decade there were some 500 in Greater London alone. The espresso machine (invented by Achille Gaggia in 1946) had virtually become a symbol of rebellious youth. Produced in Holland, this Nockit Atomic Espresso Machine (left) is made from aluminium, glass and Bakelite and dates from the mid-1950s. For the home coffee drinker there were fashionable alternatives. The coffee percolator (left) was designed in America and produced for the British market by Proctor Silex in 1959. Its star decorated glass and internal lighting illuminated the coffee and created a rich amber glow and a rocket-like effect.

Espresso machine **£150–200** *Percolator* **£50–70**

◄ John Pemberton, an Atlanta pharmacist, invented the famous Coca Cola formula in 1886. According to its original label, Coca Cola was not only a "temperance drink" and "a delicious, exhilarating... beverage" but "a valuable brain tonic and a cure for all nervous affectations". By 1950 Coca Cola made up nearly 50% of all soft drink sales in the United States and was being exported across the world. The decade saw a huge expansion in demand for soft drinks, resulting in large advertising campaigns and the production of much promotional material. This tray advertising Coca-Cola dates from 1950. Coca Cola memorabilia is highly collectable but beware of reproductions, particularly in the area of metal trays. The market is strongest in the United States, which boasts a number of collectors clubs and even a Coca Cola Museum in Elizabeth Town, Kentucky.
£70–90

► This cardboard shop display for Batchelors soup dates from the 1950s. The decade saw the launch in Britain of many now-standard convenience foods, ranging from the tea bag, introduced by Tetley's in 1953, to the fish finger, brought out by Birdseye two years later. Advertisements promised the end of tiresome chopping and cleaning, and also stressed another advantage close to the hearts of housewives who still remembered rationing – with ready-made products you could consume everything, not a single scrap of waste had to be thrown away.
£8–10

◄ This collection of tins from the 1950s sums up some of the favourite decorative themes of the period. The "pin-up" tin was made for Thornton's toffee; the triangular box contained Huntley & Palmer's Cocktail Snacks. Keiller's "portable radio" (complete with twiddling dial) was designed to contain sweets whilst Rowntree's chocolate tin commemorates the Coronation in 1953. The tin pub tray at the back is decorated with a variety of beer labels. As with pre-war tins, the more interesting the shape and the more decorative the image, the higher the value, and since these objects were mass-produced, good condition is crucial.

Pin-up tin **£18–22** Triangular tin **£10–12**
Radio tin **£22–26** Coronation tin **£6–8**
Tray **£10–12**

American Ceramics

Russel Wright (1904–76) was a leading light of the American ceramics industry. His American Modern dinnerware was launched in 1939 and dominated the market for the next 20 years, becoming one of the best-selling dinner services of all times. "Good design is for everyone", declared Wright. Working in every medium from metal to plastic, he sought to bring quality to mass-produced domestic goods and pioneered a more relaxed and informal lifestyle. American Modern, with its organic shapes and unusual mix-and-match colours, was well-suited to the contemporary home and had a seminal influence on tableware design both in the United States and abroad. The boom in post-war consumerism also stimulated demand for decorative ceramics. The properties of clay lend themselves to creating exotic and extravagent forms: ceramic television lamps became leaping panthers, ashtrays turned into abstract shapes and nubile pin-up girls. As well as tasteful functionalism, fun and fantasy also feature in 1950s American ceramics and these exuberant creations are as eagerly collected today as the great design classics.

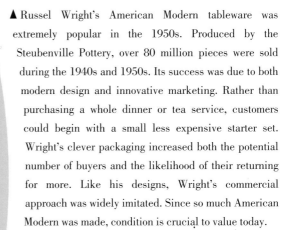

▲ Russel Wright's American Modern tableware was extremely popular in the 1950s. Produced by the Steubenville Pottery, over 80 million pieces were sold during the 1940s and 1950s. Its success was due to both modern design and innovative marketing. Rather than purchasing a whole dinner or tea service, customers could begin with a small less expensive starter set. Wright's clever packaging increased both the potential number of buyers and the likelihood of their returning for more. Like his designs, Wright's commercial approach was widely imitated. Since so much American Modern was made, condition is crucial to value today.

Teapot **£120–150** *Jug & sugar bowl* **£20–25**
Cup & saucer **£15–18**

▼ This Fiestaware jug was designed by Frederick Hurten Rhead (1880–1942). Fiestaware was first produced by the Homer Laughlin China Company, Ohio, in 1936, but like American Modern, the design was mass-produced throughout the 1950s. It was redesigned in 1960, discontinued *c.*1972 and reintroduced in 1986. The orange ceramic container was produced by the Hall China Company and made for Westinghouse. Designed for use in the refrigerator, it was given free with new appliances.

Jug **£75–85**
Covered dish **£30–40**

► Founded in Illinois in 1871, the Haeger factory introduced their Royal Haeger line in 1938. This pierced vase, fish-shaped jug and heart-shaped ashtray were produced in the 1950s by Royal Haeger. The company specialized in "art" pottery and lamp bases. Ceramics were decorated in brilliant colours; shapes were inspired by figures, animals and abstract forms interpreted in a populist style. As well as vases, and domestic wares, the factory produced a wide range of ornaments, television lamps and planters. Period catalogues also list items such as "portable fountains" and "musical flower vases", clearly aimed at the novelty market.

Vase **£70–80** *Jug* **£60–70** *Ashtray* **£40–50**

◄ Born in Switzerland in 1906, Hedi Schoop worked as a dancer in Germany until 1933 when she fled to America to escape the Nazi regime. Her new career began by chance. In 1938 she decorated some plaster dolls; a Los Angeles store suggested that she turn these creations into ceramics. Schoop set up a pottery, orders flowed in and, from the late 1940s until the pottery burnt down in 1958, Hedi Schoop Art Creations turned out an average of 30,000 objects a year. Her speciality was figurines, like these here, hand-painted, gold-sprinkled and reflecting Schoop's theatrical past in their animated poses. This giftware inspired many imitators. Original pieces are usually signed and are popular with American collectors.

Small figurine **£85–95** *Pair of figures/vases* **£375–425**

► This ashtray dates from the 1950s. It reflects not only contemporary interest in the glamour girl, but also the period fashion for home crafts. The ceramic ashtray was sold as a blank (undecorated piece) and then decorated by its purchaser. Similar examples can be found in many different colours, often signed and dated by the "artist". The growth of leisure time in the 1950s stimulated a matching development in leisure pursuits. Arts and crafts were popular hobbies, most strikingly demonstrated by the introduction in the early 1950s of the painting by numbers kit craze which swept America.

£40–48

British Ceramics

Until the early 1950s ceramic production was extremely limited in Britain. Decorative ceramics were reserved for export and the home market had to make do with serviceable, but uninspiring utility ceramics. When restrictions were finally lifted in 1952, a lust for colour and pattern reasserted itself. Plates printed with images of Paris brought a bit of continental glamour and young married couples (the major purchasers of crockery) were tempted away from traditional services by streamlined designs with abstract patterns and contemporary names. Midwinter called their new ranges "Stylecraft" and "Fashion". "You may 'fashion style' your table with the latest tableware just as you would buy the latest style in dress design", stated Roy Midwinter. Other firms limited their experiments to decorative items, particularly vases. The multiplicity of designs was partly inspired by the craze for flower arranging. "Each year sees more clubs form and more ladies take up the art. It is extremely stimulating for the creative woman... it will satisfy her sense of the dramatic", noted a contributor to Julia Clements' *Floral Roundabout* in 1959. Manufacturers sought to match these creative and dramatic urges with suitably inventive receptacles, and vases were designed in every conceivable size, shape and colour.

▲ While many manufacturers adopted asymmetry as a decorative pattern, Arthur Hallam (c.1912–76) created exuberantly abstract shapes in these designs for Beswick from the mid-1950s. The vases are dynamic in form with angled lips. Designed by Jim Hayward (b.1910), the black and white striped pattern was a period favourite, contrasting boldly here with primary colours. Beswick ceramics are becoming very collectable today.

Space capsule vase **£20–30** *Handled vase* **£25–35**
Round vase **£8–12** *Tall vase* **£45–55**

▼ The influence of television in the 1950s even extended into ceramics. Made by Beswick, this oval plate and teacup was known as a "telly set", designed to be used while watching television. The transfer printed design depicts a circus scene. Like the ballet, the circus was a popular theme in post-war decorative arts.

£12–15

▶This Fantasia side plate was designed in 1959 by Harold Bennett for the Middleport firm of Burgess & Leigh. Fantasia came in fashionable black and white, the pattern depicts the abstract shapes of contemporary tableware, using a spindly graphic line. Like images of food, domestic motifs appear throughout the decorative arts of the period. Designers celebrated the abundance of everyday goods and the excitement of new products that became available once post-war restrictions were finally lifted.

£6–8

◀This coffee set dates from *c*.1959 and was produced by the British Anchor Pottery Company (1884–1982). The poodle was a favourite motif of the decade, reflecting fascination with all things French, elegant and at the same time whimsical.

£24–28

▶In the 1930s Carlton was well-known for producing colourful decorative ceramics modelled like leaves and embossed with flowers. In the post-war period colours became less spring-like and lines grew simpler. These examples date from the 1950s. Though retaining a naturalistic form, the leaf-shaped dishes (top right) are more autumnal in feeling, more "windswept" in design than their brightly coloured predecessors. In the pair of cocktail dishes (bottom right), the leaf has resolved into an abstract form, the use of streamlined shapes and two tone colours, black and acid green, reflecting a move away from prettiness.

Leaf-shaped dishes **£36–42** *Cocktail set* **£10–14**

►Rather than expressing contemporary taste in an abstract style, plates by the Arthur Meakin factory were decorated with representational and cheerfully escapist scenes. The black and white design on this plate shows a continental street scene, starring the inevitable lady with a poodle. Today, dealers and collectors are becoming more interested in Arthur Meakin ceramics from the 1950s and prices are gradually beginning to rise.

£6–10

◄▼ Midwinter (founded in 1910) was perhaps the most innovative British ceramic factory of the 1950s. Inspired by contemporary ceramics from the United States, Roy Midwinter (1923–90) launched the Stylecraft range in 1953, followed by the Fashion line in 1954. Both were retailed under the name of Midwinter Modern, bringing organic shapes and contemporary patterns to everyday tableware. Roy Midwinter commissioned a number of artists to create designs for the factory, but the firm's resident designer was the talented Jessie Tait (b.1928). Throughout the 1950s Tait devised dozens of imaginative, predominantly abstract, patterns for Midwinter Modern. Many of her designs influenced rival potteries, for example, the black and white Zambezi pattern (left) which generated a host of zebra-striped followers. This selection of Tait's Midwinter designs includes, from top to bottom: Gay Gobbler plate, dating from 1956; Zambezi dinner plate (1956); a trio set (cup, saucer and teaplate) in the highly popular Primavera pattern (1954); Red Domino dinner plate (1953). The jauntily named Gay Gobbler plate is rarer than the others and as such is worth more in today's market.

Gay Gobbler **£40–50** *Dinner plates* **£8–12**
Primavera Trio **£28–32**

▲ ► Although only in his twenties, Sir Terence Conran (b.1931) created some of Midwinter's most exciting designs. Conran remembers Roy Midwinter as a pioneering figure, battling to persuade the chain stores "that there could be life beyond tea roses. I think he recognized in me somebody who was also bubbling with frustration and who was a sort of kindred spirit", wrote Conran in the foreword to Alan Peat's *Midwinter – A Collector's Guide* (1992). This selection of Conran's Midwinter designs includes a Chequers plate (1957), a Nature Study cup and saucer (1955) and a Stylecraft plate decorated with the Plantlife pattern (1956).

Chequers plate **£25–30** *Cup & saucer* **£8–10** *Plantlife plate* **£25–30**

◄ Roy Midwinter was eager to cover as much of the market as possible and recruited artists and designers working in a wide variety of styles. Celebrated bird painter and naturalist Sir Peter Scott (1909–89), son of the polar explorer, produced the Wild Geese pattern for Midwinter in 1955, illustrated here on this cruet set.

£30–35

► This Midwinter coffee pot and partitioned serving dish are decorated with the Cannes pattern by architect and watercolourist Sir Hugh Casson (b.1910). He had never designed for china before and found it difficult to draw something that had to fit on a teapot. Nevertheless, Casson's delicate free-hand illustrations, inspired by a trip to the south of France, resulted in Midwinter's best-selling Riviera line (1954). The Cannes pattern was produced again in 1960.

Dish **£15–20**

Coffee pot **£40–45**

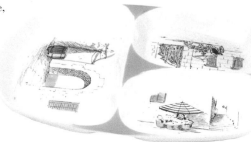

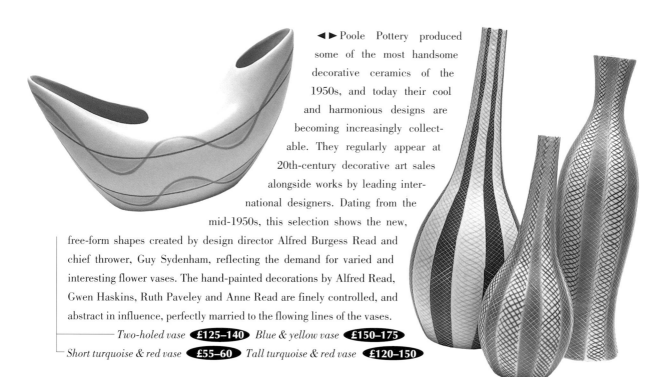

◄► Poole Pottery produced some of the most handsome decorative ceramics of the 1950s, and today their cool and harmonious designs are becoming increasingly collectable. They regularly appear at 20th-century decorative art sales alongside works by leading international designers. Dating from the mid-1950s, this selection shows the new, free-form shapes created by design director Alfred Burgess Read and chief thrower, Guy Sydenham, reflecting the demand for varied and interesting flower vases. The hand-painted decorations by Alfred Read, Gwen Haskins, Ruth Paveley and Anne Read are finely controlled, and abstract in influence, perfectly married to the flowing lines of the vases.

Two-holed vase **£125–140**   *Blue & yellow vase* **£150–175**
Short turquoise & red vase **£55–60**   *Tall turquoise & red vase* **£120–150**

▼ In the 1930s brothers Wally and John Cole were sculptors and studio potters. "Why don't you produce something good that I could use rather than putting in a showcase?" complained W. B. Honey who was both a customer and Curator of Ceramics at the Victoria and Albert Museum. This chance remark was the impetus behind Rye Pottery, which Wally and John bought in 1947. "We set out to make decent wares that could be used on the table, that was affordable and that nobody else was producing", explains Wally Cole today. Though the factory made some studio ceramics, their stock in trade during the 1950s was domestic items, such as the examples illustrated here. Made from traditional tin-glazed earthenware, each piece was well crafted and hand-painted with bright colours and abstract surface designs. "We tried to bring craft and artistry to everyday pottery", concludes Cole. Shown at the Festival of Britain and retailed though stores such as Heals in London and Tiffany of New York, today Rye's everyday pots are inspiring growing interest amongst collectors.

Two-handled vase **£40–50**   *Cruet set* **£25–30**
Avocado dish & Jug **£30–40**

◄Manufactured by Wade in the 1950s, this free-form vase expresses the contemporary fascination with space-age imagery that shot, rocket-like, across the decorative arts. This space-influenced, pierced design was enhanced by a shooting star decoration that makes it more desirable and valuable than the plain coloured versions of the same design, which Wade also produced.

£40–50

►This earthenware teaplate was produced by Swinnertons Limited (1906–59). The underglaze pattern is entitled Springtime. Set against a city background, the cartouches tell a continental love story: girl walks poodle, girl loses poodle, man finds poodle, man and poodle find girl, and the happy couple end up sitting in a café with the dog that brought them together: romance on a plate.

£3–5

◄Designed by Enid Seeney (b.1932), this Homemaker plate is probably the best known of the period. Homemaker tableware was produced by Ridgway Potteries Limited and sold exclusively through Woolworth's between 1955–67. The black and white pattern provides a ceramic catalogue of modern home furnishings including: boomerang-shaped table; Gordon Russell-style sideboard; Robin Day-influenced armchair; two-seater Bernadotte sofa; leggy plant stands; and tripod lights. These plates were produced in their thousands and are still easily found today.

£8–10

►In the 1930s artist and illustrator Eric Ravilious (1903–42) was commissioned by Wedgwood to create decorations for ceramics. During World War II he died in an aircraft accident. In the 1950s Wedgwood reissued many of his designs, whose graphic, linear style had anticipated the flavour of the new decade. This Queensware mug was originally created for the coronation of Edward VIII in 1936. Owing to the abdication, the ceremony never took place, but the design was not wasted. It was modified for the coronation of George VI, and adapted in a different colour (as shown here) for the coronation of Elizabeth II in 1953. Many ceramics were produced to celebrate this royal occasion, Wedgwood's being among the most collectable.

£200–250

European Ceramics

After World War II Picasso began to experiment with pottery. Fascinated by the new medium, he created thousands of different pieces. His work influenced designers across Europe and reflects the close relationship during the 1950s between art and craft. In Italy sculptors experimented with clay and potters explored contemporary art, using brilliant glazes, many different textures and modernist decoration. Many of the ceramics produced came from small workshops. Even the humblest, unmarked tableware can have a painterly, hand-crafted quality and prices can be surprisingly low. In Scandinavia the ceramics industry was dominated by major factories, whose products were exported around the world. Writing in the *Studio* magazine in the 1950s, Ake. H. Huldt attributed the quality of Scandinavian domestic design to a "poor, barren" landscape and a cold and dangerous climate: "our homes have always be centre of our existence. In ceramics, as in other media, Scandinavia excelled in producing everyday products that were elegant to look at and easy to live with.

▶ Pablo Picasso (1881–1973) conceived the idea for *Chouette de Femme* (Wood Owl Woman) in 1951. The pot is stamped *Edition Picasso Madoura plein feu* on the base, and is part of a limited edition of 500 vases produced by the pottery under the artist's supervision. Picasso never learned how to use the potter's wheel himself, preferring to apply his decoration to ceramic forms that had been made to his specifications. The owl shape was a favourite form, to which he returned on several occasions.

£4000–5000

◀ A highly prolific decorative artist, Piero Fornasetti (1913–88) produced a vast number of designs for printed plates and tableware during the 1950s. The Italian designer drew his imagery from an eclectic range of sources. Renaissance art was a favourite theme. This plate, which forms part of the Pittori Italiani series, shows a portrait of Paolo Ucello (1396/7–1475), Florentine painter and master of perspective, surrounded by the tools of his trade.

£150–180

▶ Italian ceramicist Marcello Fantoni (b.1915) created colourful and often sculptural ceramics. This lamp base flares out at the sides and is decorated with the incised figure of a knight on a steed. The decoration is broken up into patches of coloured enamels. The design reflects Fantoni's interest in mythological and historical imagery which emerged in his work during the 1950s.

£150–200

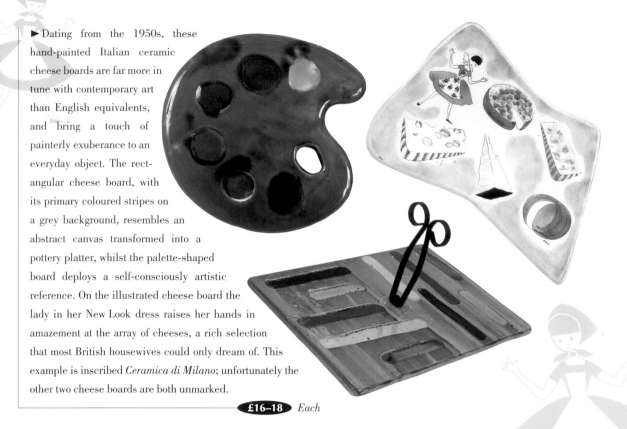

►Dating from the 1950s, these hand-painted Italian ceramic cheese boards are far more in tune with contemporary art than English equivalents, and bring a touch of painterly exuberance to an everyday object. The rect-angular cheese board, with its primary coloured stripes on a grey background, resembles an abstract canvas transformed into a pottery platter, whilst the palette-shaped board deploys a self-consciously artistic reference. On the illustrated cheese board the lady in her New Look dress raises her hands in amazement at the array of cheeses, a rich selection that most British housewives could only dream of. This example is inscribed *Ceramica di Milano*; unfortunately the other two cheese boards are both unmarked.

£16–18 *Each*

◄This striped pottery jug, with its twisted handle, reflects the interest of Italian ceramicists in exploring the effects of texture. Artists such as Guido Gambone (1909–69), founder of the Faenzerella pottery in Vietri, Italy, experimented with the three-dimensional quality of ceramics not just in terms of form but surface, using thick bubbled glazes. Gambone's work can sell for hundreds of pounds. However, like much studio pottery, this jug is unmarked and its value is considerably lower. The colourful hand-painted jug is marked Desimone 22. The clown-like figure shows the influence of Picasso, whose imagery and graphic style were echoed by potters across Europe.

£25–35 *Each*

◄The Swedish pottery Gustavsberg was internationally renowned and after World War II Stig Lindberg (1916–82) became one of their most important designers. This *Lov* (leaf) dish is typical of Lindberg's work for the factory during the early 1950s. He created a wide range of leaf-inspired vessels veined with bands of colour. The vase also has a naturalistic motif, being decorated with stylized sycamore seedpods in shades of yellow and blue, reflecting the artist's use of subtly balanced tones. After the restrictions of the war, there was a tremendous desire for colour that was underlined by a developing interest in colour psychology. Both pieces are marked with the same distinctive hand-painted monogram, as shown here.

£50–75 *Each*

►Contemporary art was an important influence on many Scandinavian designers of the period. Dating from the 1950s and made from chamotte earthenware, with glazed slip and painted decoration, this bottle-shaped vase was designed by Mari Simmulson (b.1911) for the Swedish firm Upsala-Ekeby. The long-necked lady and stylized bird recall the imagery of Picasso.

£60–80

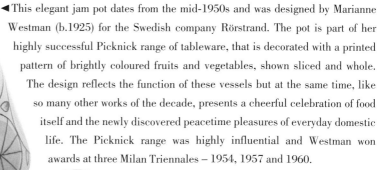

◄This elegant jam pot dates from the mid-1950s and was designed by Marianne Westman (b.1925) for the Swedish company Rörstrand. The pot is part of her highly successful Picknick range of tableware, that is decorated with a printed pattern of brightly coloured fruits and vegetables, shown sliced and whole. The design reflects the function of these vessels but at the same time, like so many other works of the decade, presents a cheerful celebration of food itself and the newly discovered peacetime pleasures of everyday domestic life. The Picknick range was highly influential and Westman won awards at three Milan Triennales – 1954, 1957 and 1960.

£16–18

► Norway was responsible for creating a number of handsome and practical designs in ceramic tableware during the 1950s. The circular dish with handle is inscribed Bambus, Ildfast, Norway. The oval plate, with its brightly coloured abstract pattern, was produced by the Egersund factory. The tureen in the middle was made by the Figgjo Fajansefabrik pottery as part of their A La Carte range. The base is marked with "Decor in underglaze quality, for Gas and Electricity, Vitrified body", reflecting the demand for ovenware that was good-looking enough to go from stove to dining table, a criterion that was admirably met by the Scandinavian potteries.

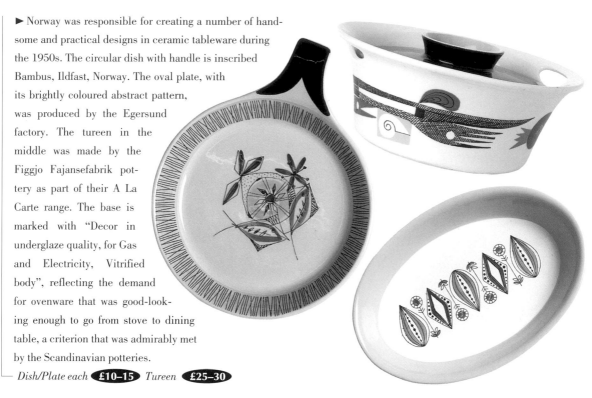

Dish/Plate each **£10–15** *Tureen* **£25–30**

◄These ceramic figures and vase were made in West Germany. The vase is quite large, measuring 13½in (34cm) high and is 23½in (60cm) in diameter. Decorated with a picture of a young couple, dressed in the latest teenage fashions, it is very representative of the 1950s. The boy is wearing tight black trousers and a brightly coloured casual jacket. The girl is dressed in a New Look skirt and an off-the-shoulder blouse, her feet encased in flat pumps and her hair in a ponytail. The small ceramic figures also date from the 1950s. These cheap and cheerful ornaments were widely exported across Europe, appearing in different forms, but with the same black and yellow decoration.

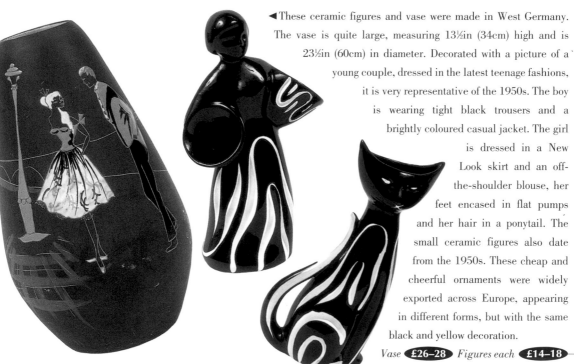

Vase **£26–28** *Figures each* **£14–18**

Italian Glass

The 1950s saw a remarkable flowering of Italian glass, which was centred around the traditional glass-making region of Murano. Venetian designers combined modern shapes with traditional techniques and brilliant colours to create glass of astonishing variety, verve and beauty. Paolo Venini (1895–1959), a lawyer turned glass maker, founded the best-known factory of the decade, and his fanciful "handkerchief" vase was to become a leitmotif of 1950s style, copied all over the world. Other influential figures include Dino Martens, Ercole Barovier and Flavio Poli. Glass by these major artists can command an international clientele and price ranges normally reserved for painting or sculpture. Good quality non-designer pieces from the 1950s are also rising in value and can fetch hundreds of pounds. However, not all Murano glass is high art and good craftmanship. A vast array of colourful and decorative glassware was produced for Venice's tourist market – gaping fish, contorted vases and endless glass clowns. Although inexpensive to begin with, these objects remain affordable today and are popular with collectors of kitsch.

◄These Occhi vases were designed for Venini c.1959 by Tobia Scarpa (b.1935). The complex decorative technique was developed by Tobia's father, architect and glass designer Carlo Scarpa. The vases are built up in a pattern of irregular tesserae, each with a central square or "eye" of clear crystal, framed by a layer of opaque, coloured glass. Tobia Scarpa also became known for his furniture designs. As with all the glass shown, value depends not only on quality but also on quality. These examples are flawless.

£2000–4000 *Each*

► Fulvio Bianconi (b.1915) had worked as an illustrator and cartoonist before turning his attentions to glass. Employed by Venini in 1947, he became one of the factory's most creative designers. This vase dates from the 1950s; its fluid line reflects the fashion for organic shapes, the striped coloured panels creating an abstract pattern. Of all media, glass is perhaps best suited to creating the asymmetric forms of 1950s style.

£3000–4000

► A painter and a designer for the glass-works of Aureliano Toso, Dino Martens (1894–1970) was responsible for some of the most colourfully inventive glass of the decade. This patchwork vase uses brilliant primary tones in a rich and painterly style. Irregular patches of pure colour are interspersed with stripes of *latticino* surrounding a central pin-wheel motif of contrasting canes.

£1800–2000

▲ In 1949 Paolo Venini and Fulvio Bianconi devised their famous *Coppa a Fazzoletto* or handkerchief bowls, created from squares of glass folded up like a piece of material. These undulating wavy-edged vessels were decorated in a variety of different techniques ranging from lace-like *latticino* to clear coloured overlay and they came in several sizes. One of the classic designs of the decade, they also inspired numerous copies (see p.71), both in Italy and abroad. The example featured here is an original Venini vase dating from the early 1950s.

£650–750

◄ Ansulo Fuga (b.1915), designer for AVEM (Arte Vetraria Muranese), created a series of highly original glass designs during the 1950s. Measuring 20in (51cm) high, this large vase with its pierced hole reflects the influence of contemporary sculpture and the work of artists such as Barbara Hepworth and Henry Moore. The patchwork decoration is comprised of compressed, multi-coloured canes, opaque white glass and a layer of coloured glass, and the vase dates from *c.*1955.

£3000–4000

► Dating from 1954, this Neolitici vase was designed by Ercole Barovier (1889–1974). In contrast to the bright colours popular with many designers, Barovier experimented with subdued shades such as greens and browns. Delicate patterns were obtained by using difficult techniques, here *graffito*, in which the glass was combed in order to create the festooned pattern. The glass produced by the Barovier & Toso factory, rivalled Venini in its inventiveness.

£1800–2000

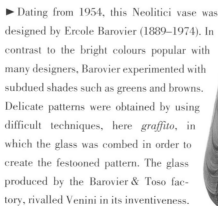

►Flavio Poli (1900–84) has been described as the most Nordic of the Venetian glass makers, with his predilection for strong organic forms, enhanced by brilliant colours. This long-necked bottle and heart-shaped vase belong to the Valva series, based on shell forms and produced *c.*1956 for Seguso Vetri d'Arte. Poli was a great master of the *sommerso* technique, creating vessels from thick, transparent layers of glass, superimposed one over the other. The contrasting lines of clear and coloured crystal emphasize the abstracted design. After completion each piece would be painstakingly polished to remove the slightest irregularity. Large in size and, thanks to the cased glass, extremely heavy, the literal monumentality of these vessels is reflected in the simple clarity of their sculptural design.

£500–800 *Each*

▼ Although not by well-known designers, these three pieces are high in quality; the cased glass is clear and heavy, with luminous colours and a strong design. The green Seguso vase with its flared neck and asymmetric mouth is typical of the period. The Murano ducks reflect the more fanciful side of Venetian taste, many of the best and the worst Italian glass makers experimenting with playful animal and figurative forms.

Ducks **£200–250**

Vase **£300–400**

◄ As well as decorative vases, figures and statuettes were also extremely popular Murano tourist items. These examples include a cockerel, a lady in vaguely historical dress and a clown – a favourite subject whose colourful form appears in endless, grimacing variations.

£20–25 *Each*

► These vases belong to the tourist end of the Murano market. The colours are flat, the weight comparatively light, and the shapes twisted into almost a parody of contemporary free-form styling. Nevertheless, on their own level, they capture spirit of the 1950s as much as some the finest Italian glass of the period and they are far less expensive.

£35–55 *Each*

◄ Glass fish were produced in shoals of thousands by the Italian glassworks in the 1950s and 1960s. Like many other decorative objects of the period, they have suffered from the vagaries of fashion, moving from being seen as a popular decorative object to the epitome of vulgar bad taste to an amusing and collectable example of 1950s kitsch (see pp.74–5). One generation bought them new, the following generation slung them out in disgust and today's generation (the grandchildren) are buying them back from antique shops.

£10–20

Scandinavian Glass

The Scandinavian countries were leading producers of glass during the 1950s. At the beginning of the decade Finland emerged from the deprivations and isolation of World War II to score an immense triumph at the Milan Triennale of 1951. Their display won six Grand Prix awards, along with a host of other medals, and Finnish design was exported around the world. Critics have often stressed the influence of the landscape on Finnish designers, particularly in the studio glass of Tapio Wirkkala (1915–85) and Timo Sarpaneva (b.1926), whose sculptural creations for Iittala in icy crystal were inspired by both abstract and natural forms. Iittala was the most famous glassworks in Finland. Other major manufacturers included Nuutajärvi, where designer Kaj Franck (b.1911) created works of colourful and rational elegance. In Sweden, the Orrefors factory nurtured many important designers, including Sven Palmqvist (1906–84), Ingeborg Lundin (b.1921) and Edvin Öhrström (b.1906). At the Kosta glassworks, Vicke Lindstrand (1904–83) used luminous colours, worthy of Murano, but with a typically Swedish control. Scandinavian glass is generally more restrained compared to the bright tones of Italian glass and often less expensive.

► Painter and sculptor, Timo Sarpaneva produced designs for everything from textiles to saucepans, but it was for glass that he became most celebrated. Sarpaneva started work at Iittala in 1950. This Orchid vase (c.1957) was conceived of as a piece of sculpture – an elongated bubble of air, pierced at the centre and captured in a smooth oval piece of heavy crystal. Sarpaneva experimented with abstract forms, exploring the relationship between mass and void using the transparent properties of glass. The Orchid series was first produced in 1954.

£400–600

◄ This vase was designed by Kaj Franck, one of Finland's most eminent designers. Like many Scandinavian artists, he worked in a variety of media, producing both industrial designs as well as one-off, hand-made pieces. In the 1950s Franck designed the inexpensive, mix-and-match coloured Kilta tableware for the ceramics company Arabia, which was to become the everyday staple of most Finnish homes. This heavy cased-glass vase, created for Nuutajärvi-Notsjo, belongs to the more exclusive, craft-based side of his work. However, it still reflects the interest in clean lines and contrasting colours that infuses his most functional pieces.

£350–450

► Having worked at the Orrefors factory, Vicke Lindstrand moved to the Kosta glassworks in 1950. He produced a huge variety of glass. This example shows his interest in strong colours and subtle decoration, the delicate movement of spiralling blue threads held in check by the supporting frame of clear cased glass.

£200–300

◄This pink glass vase, cased in clear crystal and decorated with bands of air bubbles, was created by architect, potter and glass designer Gunnar Nylund (b.1904). In 1954 he was appointed artistic director of the Swedish Strömbergshyttan glass factory. Nylund was interested in exploring the possibilities of organic shapes and the decorative potential of cased glass – not surprisingly his works are sculptural in style. "Glass will express so much more than the other materials," claimed fellow Swedish glass designer Sven Palmqvist, "it will never be affected, it is eternal, unchangeable, the air bubble born in the heat of a sudden improvisation, locked up forever in the crystal block – a moment of eternity in the wide space of the universe."

£350–450

► Edvin Öhrström, whose works are highly prized today, designed this Ariel vase. The term Ariel refers to the decorative technique that Öhrström first developed in the 1930s. The design was cut into the basic glass vessel, then it was covered with a layer of molten glass, leaving the image suspended in an air pocket between the glass walls. Öhrström was to experiment with this technique over the next two decades. The blue, green and amber decoration inside this vase depicts a woman's head shown in profile surrounded by rosettes.

£2500–3000

▼ This bullet-shaped, blue glass vase with a bottle-green coloured well was designed in 1954 by Norwegian designer Willy Johansson for Hadeland, the glassworks that is still responsible today for most of the glassware produced in Norway. In 1954 Norway made its first appearance at the Milan Triennales where this design, along with other Johansson glassware, was awarded a diploma of honour.

£120–150

Decorative Glassware

Colourful decorated glasses were produced in their thousands in the 1950s and 1960s. Typical themes include abstract patterns, cocktail imagery, musical motifs and figurative scenes. Glasses came in multicoloured sets or with a series of related images. Although they were inexpensive, they were also fragile and complete sets are rare today, particularly those with large glasses. The more unusual designs command comparatively high prices. Individual glasses and single shot glasses, however, can be still be bought from second-hand shops and car boot sales and it is possible to make a fun, varied and usable collection for very little expense. Decorated glasses were made around the world but rarely are they marked with a name or a country of origin. Commemorative glasses celebrating the major events of the 1950s are easier to identify and are very popular today.

▼ Sets of cocktail glasses in wirework containers with cocktail cherry legs were produced in various shapes and styles during the 1950s. Stands were inset with mirrors, or even modelled in the form of gondolas or handcarts being pushed by skeletal, orientalized figures. This set of glasses with their mix-and-match colours is typical of the period and similar sets are easily found today.

£10–12

► Playing cards were a popular decorative motif of the period, turning up on a wide variety of objects from furniture to fashionable clothing. This set of glasses on a twisted metal stand comes with a matching decanter.

£18–20 *Set*

▼ Sets of glasses often featured different designs based around a single theme, such as costume through the ages and vintage cars. As in other fields, exotic and colourful subjects were often favoured and this late-1950s group shows different dances from around the world. The Western glass (far left), with its New York inspired landscape, shows rock 'n' roll, an image that began to appear increasingly on decorative items by the end of the decade.

£14–16 *Set*

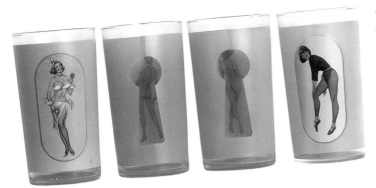

◄These glasses reflect the fashion for both pin-up material and novelty designs. Seen from the front the women are clothed, albeit scantily, turn the glasses around and a keyhole shape reveals their nude forms. A favourite subject for this treatment was women in national costume, their innocuous image adding to the surprise behind. Full sets are rare and sought after today.

£50–60 *Set*

"maximum meaning, minimum means"

►The 1951 Festival of Britain spawned a host of commemorative material which is becoming increasingly collectable today and correspondingly harder to find. These glasses are decorated with the Festival logo created by graphic artist Abram Games (1914–96). A successful designer of posters, Games created a number of powerful propaganda images during World War II, always following his personal credo of "maximum meaning, minimum means". The red, white and blue logo features the head of Britannia surrounded by pennants, its clear design capturing the patriotic and celebratory nature of the occasion. The logo became synonymous with the public conception of the Festival.

£5–10 *Each*

◄These glasses record another major festival of the 1950s, the Brussels Universal and International Exhibition of 1958. Celebrating the atomic age, the exhibition took science as its main inspiration, and events included the first public demonstration of Nuclear Fission as well as the latest information on the space race. The glasses are decorated with the exhibition's logo and the form of the Atomium, the huge and magnificent building in Brussels modelled on the image of an iron molecule (see p.13).

(see p.13)

£5–10 *Each*

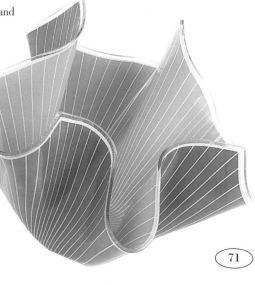

►The British glass company Chance was one of the many firms to emulate Venini's famous handkerchief vases. Whereas the Italian originals have a fluid, lace-like quality, their imitators often have the appearance of starched and folded napkins, as this example demonstrates.

£10–12

Plastics

Plastic revolutionized the look of the 1950s home. Manufacturers of laminated surfaces and vinyl flooring promised housewives a work-free and colourful existence. "The cheering colours of Formica beckon you to an everyday life that is free from needless drudgery", boasted a typical advertisement. Having been liberated from housework, housewives were then encouraged to redecorate so as the industry would benefit from the development of the profitable DIY market. "Fablon transforms your home. Give the kitchen table a new gleaming surface. Go gay with Fablon", said another advertisement. "Gay" was the adjective often used by manufacturers of melamine tableware, which was promoted as low in price, bright in colour and perfect for use with children. Plastics reflected the fashion for a more informal relaxed lifestyle, pioneered in the domestic products of Charles Eames and Russel Wright. Today there is a market both for designer wares and the fun plastics of the 1950s, perhaps best summed up by that icon of kitsch, the pineapple ice bucket.

▲ In 1953 American designer Russel Wright launched his melamine Residential tableware. The properties of plastic lent themselves perfectly to Wright's predilection for fluid, organic forms. Residential tableware came in a range of modern colours with a lightly mottled finish. Whereas plastics were often thought of as being an inexpensive alternative to ceramics, Residential was designed to be used at dining tables as well as the family kitchen: "Elegance in dinnerware", boasted the advertisements,"richly textured colours, never before contours". The service was given an official seal of approval in 1953 when it won the Museum of Modern Art's Good Design Award.

Jug **£30–35** *Plates, Cups & saucers, Bowls* **£16–18**

◄ Melamine was developed during the 1930s, but was not used in the domestic market until after World War II. Because melamine can take strong dyes, it encouraged the fashion for brightly coloured mix-and-match tableware, which was marketed as being both fun and unbreakable. Advertisements often featured cups and plates being dropped to no ill-effect by clumsy husbands and children, underlying their advantage over ceramics. A number of British companies manufactured melamine tableware, including Midwinter. These colourful cups were part of the Melaware range of tableware, produced by the British firm Ranton and Company.

£5 *Each*

►The fashion for cocktails inspired many plastic extravagances. The pineapple ice bucket (this example has an interior glass liner) was a favourite conceit of the 1950s and 1960s, another popular, fruity shape being the apple ice bucket. The "whistle for your drink" cocktail mixers are made from glitter plastic, each one with a tiny plastic whistle, the container enticing drinkers to "wet your whistle". It is rare to find both contents and packaging complete, particularly given the ephemeral nature of these party items. The pineapple ice bucket is a far more commonplace object and, consequently, less expensive.

Ice bucket **£8–10**   *Mixers* **£18–20**

"wet your whistle"

◄Acrylic, the transparent plastic best known under the trade names Lucite and Perspex, provided the material for some of the most whimsical creations of the post-World War II period. It was used for handbags and shoes, as well as for producing highly decorative domestic products. This Dreamlight table lamp dating from the 1950s is made of etched and engraved Perspex. It reflects the contemporary taste for asymmetric shapes and fantasy designs.

£140–170

►Plastic was the perfect material for outdoor use. Dating from the 1950s, these colourful basket-weave chairs pierced the lawns of innumerable suburban gardens with their splayed metal legs. The fashionable capsule-shaped chair (shown here in red and white) was the most common design, and period examples are easily found today. The child's rocker and the curved triangle chair are more unusual, hence their higher value.

Capsule **£15–20**   *Triangular* **£30–40**
Child's rocker **£25–35**

Fabulous Kitsch

The Oxford English Dictionary defines kitsch as *"objets d'art* characterized by worthless pretentiousness". The word dates from the 1920s, but it was in the 1950s that kitsch truly came into its own. New materials and production techniques resulted in an explosion of frivolous objects aimed at a consumer-hungry public with a lust to decorate and more money to spend than ever before. This selection illustrates a few popular favourites from the period. For some, this aspect of 1950s style is synonymous with cringeworthy bad taste, but for others it represents the ultimate in desirability. These items are undeniably kitsch, but the term is no longer just pejorative and they are certainly not worthless. There is a buoyant demand for such material, the more extravagantly tacky the better.

▲ ▶ First popularized in the 1930s, flying ducks remained popular in the 1950s and good ceramic sets from the period, such as the set illustrated, are highly sought after. Disembodied heads made from plaster (as shown here) or china were another favourite wall decoration. Popular subjects included ponytailed girls and Oriental or Nubian subjects; sets often came in his and hers pairs. Price depends on quality, material and levels of exotic fantasy.

Ducks **£55–65** *Heads* **£15–25**

▼ The enormous increase in car ownership in Britain during the 1950s had a number of consequences. The decade witnessed the introduction of parking meters, the opening of the first motorway, the unveiling of the Mini and the rise to popularity of the nodding dog on the parcel shelf. This pack dates from the 1950s and shows the contemporary preference for "cute" toy breeds, lovingly re-created with simulated, brushed nylon fur. The canine equivalent of fluffy dice, the nodding dog is often held up as the epitome of bad taste and is correspondingly popular today with collectors of kitsch. Purists might sneer, but enthusiasts maintain that nodding dogs and busty Martini shakers summon up the spirit of the period as much as a Charles Eames chair.

£5–12 *Each*

► The term pin-up apparently derives from World War II when servicemen pinned up "girlie" pictures in their quarters. The fashion for pin-up items burgeoned in the 1950s, epitomized by this battery-operated "Miss Mixer": "This go-go girl will mix well at any party! Put your drink in her attached holder, press the button and she'll really shake up a mean drink! Stirs up the drinks and the drinkers too! Take off the removable gold bikini top – Wow!" What more could a drinker want, apart from a set of Miss Busty squeezable rubber drinks coasters. Glamour material is very desirable today.

"Wow!"

— *Miss Busty* **£20–25** *Miss Mixer* **£125–150**

"Stirs up the drinks and the drinkers too!"

◄ During the 1950s, *The Chinese Girl* and an endless series of similar green ladies graced living-room walls across the world. Their creator, Vladimir Griegorovich Tretchikoff, was born in Siberia in 1913 and settled in South Africa from 1946. The self-taught painter became famous not through original canvases but thousands of reproductions, costing little and sold in chainstores everywhere. He favoured exotic subjects, bathed in a distinctive luminous glow, recalling the colour of houseflies. Although the quality of these pictures is debatable, their success is not. Tretchikoff made a fortune and was probably the most genuinely popular artist of the decade. His paintings, however, although certainly part of art history are rarely if ever mentioned in art historical accounts.

£30–35

► Cats and poodles were favourite decorative motifs. The long-necked cat became one of the design clichés of the period and today no second-hand shop is complete without a strangulated pottery feline. This group includes a cat candle with a diamanté collar. The poodle was a popular choice, appearing on everything from handbags to teacups and even gave its name to a haircut. Its popularity reflected the contemporary fascination with Paris and all things French, and a lust for frivolity. During World War II the British bulldog became a national symbol, after the conflict it was time for fun and the poodle.

£5–10 *Each*

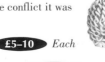

Metalware

Metal was the perfect material for moulding into contemporary shapes, be it the splayed legs of a chair or the spike of a stiletto heel. Among the most distinctive metallic products of the decade were the twisted wirework creations – plant holders, fruit bowls and magazine racks. These objects were produced in such profusion that prices remain relatively low today. In Britain innovative designs in metalware were produced by Robert Welch (b.1929), who was both a silver craftsman and an industrial designer in stainless steel. David Mellor (b.1930) pioneered simple and modern design for cutlery and tableware, his award-winning designs matching the elegant functionalism of Swedish or Norwegian products. In Scandinavia, the close relationship between art and industry affected design in every media including metal. Created in 1957, Arne Jacobsen's stainless steel AJ cutlery was modern, minimalist and economical to mass produce and it is still manufactured today. Danish designer Henning Koppel (1918–81) used his sculptural training to create jewellery and tableware that fused organic with abstract form. His creativity was matched by the Italian designer Lino Sabattini (b.1925), who wrought silverware into asymmetric shapes.

◄ This metal candelabra was made in Denmark in the 1950s. Its design is inspired by atomic and molecular diagrams, and like a puzzle the various pieces can be taken apart and put together again to create new shapes. The candelabra is both decorative and functional; the designer has come very close to creating a work of sculpture.

£100–150

▼ This silver Pride tea service was designed by David Mellor in 1959 and manufactured by Walker & Hall. The Pride range of tableware and cutlery, produced both in silver and EPNS, was a critical and commercial success. This set received the Council for Industrial Design Award in 1959. David Mellor is an extremely versatile designer. Commissions in the 1960s ranged from the silver tableware used in British Embassies around the globe to the low-cost, stainless steel Thrift cutlery destined for H.M. Prisons.

£1500–2000

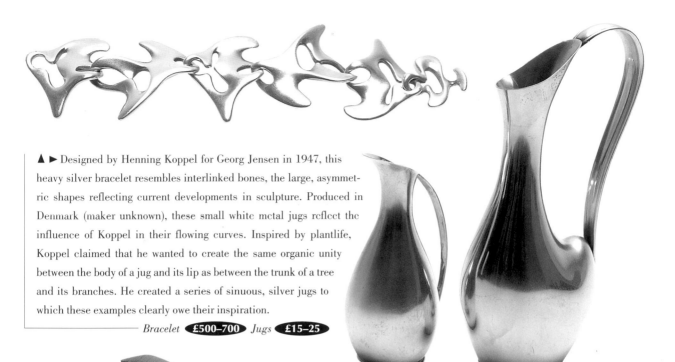

▲ ► Designed by Henning Koppel for Georg Jensen in 1947, this heavy silver bracelet resembles interlinked bones, the large, asymmetric shapes reflecting current developments in sculpture. Produced in Denmark (maker unknown), these small white metal jugs reflect the influence of Koppel in their flowing curves. Inspired by plantlife, Koppel claimed that he wanted to create the same organic unity between the body of a jug and its lip as between the trunk of a tree and its branches. He created a series of sinuous, silver jugs to which these examples clearly owe their inspiration.

Bracelet **£500–700** *Jugs* **£15–25**

◄ Robert Welch made his mark on the home with his stainless steel tableware. Among his first creations for the Old Hall company in 1955 was this stainless steel toast rack. In 1956 he collaborated with David Mellor to produce the Campden range, to which this wooden handled coffee pot belongs. Conceived of as competition for Scandinavian products, it won a Design Centre Award in 1958. Modern and economical, Welch's designs have a somewhat institutional feel. Those who grew up with his utilitarian products can find it hard to see them as design classics, and many who purchased his tableware in the 1950s and 1960s often discarded it in the following decades.

Coffee pot **£18–22** *Toast rack* **£10–15**

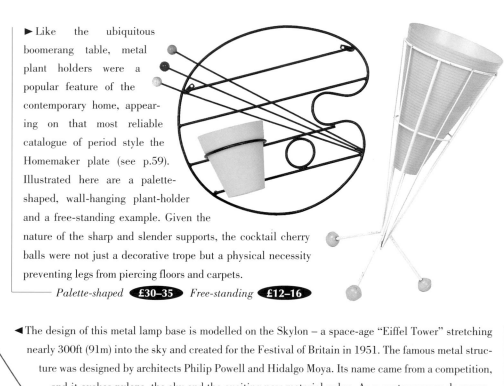

▶ Like the ubiquitous boomerang table, metal plant holders were a popular feature of the contemporary home, appearing on that most reliable catalogue of period style the Homemaker plate (see p.59). Illustrated here are a palette-shaped, wall-hanging plant-holder and a free-standing example. Given the nature of the sharp and slender supports, the cocktail cherry balls were not just a decorative trope but a physical necessity preventing legs from piercing floors and carpets.

Palette-shaped **£30–35** *Free-standing* **£12–16**

◀ The design of this metal lamp base is modelled on the Skylon – a space-age "Eiffel Tower" stretching nearly 300ft (91m) into the sky and created for the Festival of Britain in 1951. The famous metal structure was designed by architects Philip Powell and Hidalgo Moya. Its name came from a competition, and it evokes pylons, the sky and the exciting new material nylon. As a contemporary documentary film reported, the aim of the Skylon was to "hang upright in the air and astonish", capturing the spirit of the festival, "serious, witty, vulgar and even a little mad". Secured by thin cables, it seemed to stand without any visible means of support – like Britain itself, commented contemporary cynics. Tragically, after the Festival, the Skylon was scrapped, its legacy remaining in such decorative items.

£100–150

▶ This black, iron, zigzag wall tidy with its multi-coloured wooden balls is an archetypal piece of 1950s design. The decade was known as the Atomic Age, and much decorative imagery was inspired by nuclear physics and the breaking down of matter into atoms and molecules, discoveries physically expressed by lines and blobs. This wall tidy is a fine and costly example of the atomic or "cocktail cherry" style; wire and plastic versions of the same design are more common and less expensive.

£70–80

► The advantage of metal was that it could be twisted and teased into a multiplicity of fantastical shapes. This Miss Kitty letter rack is a perfect example of period whimsy; the more sophisticated examples came with a pen holder in the tail and even a sponge for stamps embedded in the cat's head. More bizarre still is the gilded wire lamp base, the eye-shaped ornament containing a surreal montage of dried flowers and real butterflies on a lacy background.

— *Miss Kitty* **£6–8** *Lamp base* **£15–20**

◄ Wire was the popular choice both for magazine and record racks (see p.35). As with the growth of magazines in the 1950s, the expansion of the music industry resulted in new storage requirements for the home. Record collections were swelled by the craze for rock 'n' roll and the host of long-playing, extended-playing and single records targeted at the new teenage market.

£5–6

► Metal was a popular choice for outdoor furniture. This Plan-O Spider chair was made in the 1950s by the French designer Hoffer for Plan. As its name suggests, the chair was inspired by a spider's web. The metal tubular frame folds flat and the seat is composed of a web-like pattern of springy elastic. A modernist deck chair par excellence, the Plan-O Spider appeared in Jacques Tati's 1958 film, *Mon Oncle*. Tati's first colour feature was a satire on the absurdities of contemporary life, contrasting the simple existence of comic hero Mr Hulot with that of his sister and brother-in-law in their ultra-modern, gadget-filled, design-crazy home.

£400–500

Textiles

The home owner who would never have hung an abstract painting on the wall was nevertheless happy to invest in colourful, contemporary curtains. "Probably everyone's boredom with wartime dreariness and lack of variety helped the establishment of this new and gayer trend", explained Lucienne Day (b.1917) in the *Daily Mail Ideal Home Book* in 1957. Lucienne, who was married to furniture designer Robin Day, was perhaps the most important textile artist of the decade. Her 1951 fabric Calyx is credited with introducing the abstract patterns that hung in windows across Britain. Firms such as Heals and David Whitehead sponsored progressive designers whose names, fortunately for collectors today, were proudly emblazoned on the selvages of their modernist fabrics. At auction, textiles by these pioneering manufacturers can fetch hundreds of pounds (particularly if not made up), yet it is still possible to pick up curtains (sometimes by named artists) for next to nothing from second-hand shops. Values depend on design, condition and size.

◄Although faded, these Calyx curtains are still desirable. The Calyx pattern was designed by Lucienne Day for the Festival of Britain (1951). Inspired by artists such as Miro and Calder, Day pioneered textile design in Britain. Calyx won awards from the American Institute of Designers and the Milan Triennale. **£90–130**

► This Hourglass textile was designed by W. Hertzberger *c*.1954 for the British firm of Turnbull and Stockdale. The colours are typical of the period and the design reflects the popularity of the hourglass shape. The material was illustrated in the *Studio Year Book 1956/57*. This fabric is 50in (127cm) wide, 3¼yd (3m) long, **£180–240**

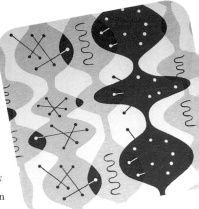

◄"Two years ago, reds, limes and yellows were hailed as brilliant, exciting and gay.... Now black supersedes the bright colours of the last few years and it will soon be seen to be exactly right for the newest ideas in interior decoration", warned the *Daily Mail Ideal Home Book* in 1955. Designed in the mid-1950s by Mary Warren for Heals, Nautilus (left) reflects the fashion for black and white and it has an equally contemporary motif. This detail is from a pair of printed curtains. **£100–150**

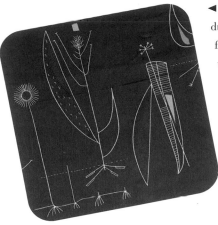

◄ Herb Anthony, illustrated here, was another Lucienne Day design, first produced for Heals in 1954. The basis of the design is a floral motif, a traditional favourite in textiles. Day transforms these flowers into spindly skeletons, flecked with bright colours and echoing the wiry forms of contemporary furnishings. This detail is taken from a pair of curtains each measuring 116in (294cm) wide by 2⅛yd (2m) long. The curtains are in perfect condition.

£200–300

► Scientific imagery was a major inspiration for 1950s designers. The designs for many products for the Festival of Britain were based on crystal structures. "They were essentially modern, because the technique that discovered them was quite recent and yet, like all successful decoration of the past, they derived from nature", explained *Design* magazine in 1951. This textile by J. Feldman for David Whitehead *c.*1954 is inspired by the shape of molecules. It is 50in (127cm) wide, 2⅜yd (2.5m) long.

£150–200

► Surrealist art was another important influence on contemporary textile design. This easy chair was manufactured by the Phoenix Chair Company, Wisconsin, USA, in the 1950s. It is upholstered in a leaf-hand pattern by Salvador Dali (1904–89), grand master and major publicist of Surrealism, who resided in the United States from 1940 to 1955 and, like many artists of the period, produced a number of designs for decorative arts. The value of this chair lies above all in its fabric cover.

£500–600

◀ These swatches come from a large group of David Whitehead samples preserved from the 1950s and recently sold at auction. The company was known for colourful, contemporary designs, produced in high-quality, hand-printed cotton and less expensive machine-printed rayon. The rose pattern, shown in three colourways, was created by Hilda Durkin; the abstract pattern was designed by Marion Mahler, one of Whitehead's most talented designers. A few years ago these fabric samples would have been virtually worthless. The value of the whole collection reflects the growing interest today in textiles from the 1950s.

£275–350 *Collection*

◀ The painter John Piper (1903–92) is best known for his romantic portrayal of English architectural sites, an interest that was enhanced by the destructive threat of World War II. He was one of many artists including, among others, Henry Moore and Eduardo Paolozzi, to design textiles. This linen fabric was produced for David Whitehead in the 1950s and measures 50in (127cm) wide, 2yd (1.8m) long.

£175–200

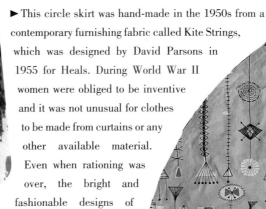

▶ This circle skirt was hand-made in the 1950s from a contemporary furnishing fabric called Kite Strings, which was designed by David Parsons in 1955 for Heals. During World War II women were obliged to be inventive and it was not unusual for clothes to be made from curtains or any other available material. Even when rationing was over, the bright and fashionable designs of furnishing textiles presented an attractive and less expensive alternative to buying ready-made clothes. Fabric from the period tends to be worth more when it has not been made up.

£35–45

◄ This American fabric reflects the fashion for wild west prints that emerged in in the 1940s and 1950s. Cowboy images were enormously popular in the period that produced Hopalong Cassidy and the Lone Ranger. The demand for western fabrics lessened in the 1960s as cowboys were superseded by a new generation of television super heroes. This single curtain is 35in (89cm) wide, 2½yd (2.3m) long.

£40–50

► These details come from two pairs of 1950s curtains purchased at a second-hand shop for very little cost. The black and white design is inscribed "Made by Cepea" along the selvage and reflects the period fascination with Paris. The abstract floral example is not marked, but its colourful rayon design is typical of the contemporary patterns produced for the popular market. Both sets of curtains are short, measuring only 50in (127cm) in length. Many curtains from the period seem to have been produced for particularly diminutive windows and most textile collectors have cupboards filled with curtains that look wonderful, but do not fit anywhere.

£20–30 *Each pair*

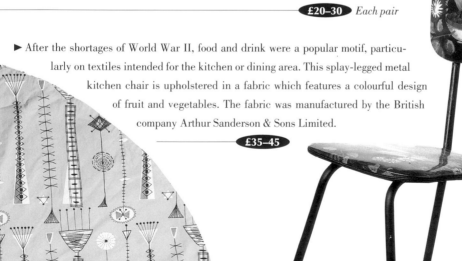

► After the shortages of World War II, food and drink were a popular motif, particularly on textiles intended for the kitchen or dining area. This splay-legged metal kitchen chair is upholstered in a fabric which features a colourful design of fruit and vegetables. The fabric was manufactured by the British company Arthur Sanderson & Sons Limited.

£35–45

fashion

"The season's sensation is the new house of Christian Dior", enthused Vogue in March 1947. After utilitarian wartime fashions, Dior's New Look was a revelation: padded jackets emphasizing bust and hips, waist-whittling corsetry and long swirling skirts, using yards of precious, rationed material. "I designed clothes for flower-like women," claimed Dior, "I brought back the neglected art of pleasing." Politicians campaigned against the waste of textiles, protesters brandished placards saying "Burn Monsieur Dior". Women, however, were entranced, and Dior's hourglass line launched a decade of feminine fashions, epitomized by the stiletto heel. This section follows 1950s style from haute couture to the high street, from the circle skirt to the circle-stitch bra. It illustrates elegant ladies' fashions and the casual look adopted by the new generation of trouser-clad teenage girls. Men's styles are featured in both formal suits and brightly-coloured leisure wear. The section concludes with the growing influence of the United States, the emergence of street style, and the introduction of denim as the international uniform of youth.

Women's Wear

Throughout the 1950s, Dior and the other great couturiers of the period introduced new collections every six months, shapes varying from flowing ball gowns to the slimmest of pencil skirts, which permitted no more than a ladylike hobble. Versions of the latest Paris fashions could be supplied to all thanks to new techniques of mass production and synthetic materials developed during World War II. Easy-care fabrics and the growing availability of washing machines and laundromats meant that everyone could have clean clothes every day and wear bright colours, luxuries formerly restricted to the rich. Influenced by the United States, the period saw a massive expansion in mix-and-match coordinates and ready-to-wear clothes. Chainstores flourished and even the most exclusive designers began to experiment with profitable *pret-à-porter* lines.

While 1950s haute couture sells for hundreds of pounds, everyday clothes from the period can be picked up for prices that match or undercut their modern equivalents. Quality tends to be good or the garments would not have survived, and with the flexibility of contemporary fashion, most of the clothes shown are wearable today.

► During the occupation of France in World War II, Christian Dior (1905–57) designed for the cinema. The film industry was controlled by the Germans who promoted non-political subjects such as costume dramas. Dior experimented with crinolines and corsets, learning the techniques that were to be the literal foundations of his post-war fashions. Crucial to this full-skirted new look was plenty of material. Textile magnate Marcel Broussac agreed to back Dior in the hope that, once rationing was over, his long styles would increase demand for material. This green silk dress is by Dior. The wide skirt is supported by a stiffened peticoat.

£300–400

► In the early 1950s Dior announced a new line that was higher waisted, narrow skirted and sinuous. This pencil-slim black velvet evening dress was made for the English ballerina Margot Fonteyn. Dior was one of her favourite designers, and much of her wardrobe is now in the collection of British museums. The shot of the tightly boned bodice shows the concealed inner structure for which the couturier was famous. Dior claimed that his clothes were "constructed like buildings", and it was said that his dresses stood up by themselves. Although this gown has an impressive provenance, its condition is poor. It was clearly much loved and often worn by its famous owner.

£375–425

◄ In 1954 Coco Chanel (1883–1971) showed her first post-war collection. She was radically opposed to Dior's structured creations. "Boned horrors, that's what they are", she told *Vogue* in 1954. "A dress isn't right if it is uncomfortable, if it doesn't 'walk' properly." Following on from her 1930s designs, Chanel's clothes from the 1950s included the simple cardigan suit which was copied in its thousands, and cocktail dresses such as this blue lace example that is lightly modelled, hard to crease and easy to wear.

£350–375

> *"A dress isn't right if it is uncomfortable, if it doesn't 'walk' properly."*

► Alongside Dior, the Spanish designer Christobal Balenciaga (1895–1972) was perhaps the most influential designer of the 1950s. His mastery was tailoring and this suit exhibits some of the features that he made famous: the box shaped, waistless jacket over a slim skirt; three-quarter length sleeves, drawing attention to the wrist; a distinctive, cut-away collar, emphasizing the length of the neck; and large, elegant buttons. The jacket has weights sewn into the lining at the sides in order to preserve a perfect line.

£475–525

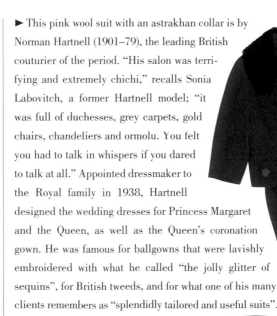

► This pink wool suit with an astrakhan collar is by Norman Hartnell (1901–79), the leading British couturier of the period. "His salon was terrifying and extremely chichi," recalls Sonia Labovitch, a former Hartnell model; "it was full of duchesses, grey carpets, gold chairs, chandeliers and ormolu. You felt you had to talk in whispers if you dared to talk at all." Appointed dressmaker to the Royal family in 1938, Hartnell designed the wedding dresses for Princess Margaret and the Queen, as well as the Queen's coronation gown. He was famous for ballgowns that were lavishly embroidered with what he called "the jolly glitter of sequins", for British tweeds, and for what one of his many clients remembers as "splendidly tailored and useful suits".

£175–225

◄ Both of these dresses are American. "Prom" or party frocks were usually full or ballerina length, made from nylon tulle, rayon chiffon and artificial lace, and came in a rainbow of colours from vibrant reds to delicate pastel shades. The layered skirts were puffed out still further by candy coloured nylon petticoats. These bouffant dresses were mass produced by a large number of manufacturers and were a favourite choice with young girls going to the hop. Given that they tended to be worn by partying teenagers, condition can be poor and it is always advisable to check for tears and other damage or staining. The skirts at the back were particularly vulnerable to being pierced by sharp stiletto heels. These two examples, however, are in perfect condition.

£40–50 *Each*

► Created by Philip Hulitar, this American yellow and gold silk gown represents a more sophisticated and glamorous look than the pretty, puff-ball "prom" dress. The sheath shape caresses the legs and hugs the hips; the strapless bodice is heavily boned and designed to show off and provide maximum support for a well developed figure. The name Conchita is inscribed in pencil on the lining. This gown could possibly have been worn by a showgirl and it certainly has a flavour of Hollywood. Similar dresses were modelled by such famous film stars as Marilyn Monroe and Jane Russell, whose celebrated cleavage attracted much admiration. "There are two good reasons why men go to see her and those are enough", boasted Russell's mentor Howard Hughes, who also claimed credit for designing her specially cantilevered and much publicized bra. Many designs of the period emphasized the bust. Dior provided "falsies" for his slender mannequins, and the 1950s was a golden age for manufacturers of underwear, who with padding, wiring and complex engineering, moulded women's bodies into fashionably prominent curves.

£90–110

◄ After the war there was a huge craving for luxury; mink was the ultimate status symbol. "The trick of wearing mink is to look as though you are wearing a cloth coat. The trick of wearing a cloth coat is to look as though you are wearing a mink", advised Pierre Balmain in 1955. Ranch breeding increased the variety and the availability of fur, which appeared in every form, from the mink coats worn by president's wife, Mamie Eisenhower, to the infamous mink bikini sported by British starlet Diana Dors (née Diana Fluck) at the Venice film festival in 1955. Reflecting contemporary fashions, this black jersey sheath dress and cashmere cardigan, made by Margulis Furs Clayton, both have real mink collars. Tastes and morals have changed, and today such fur-trimmed items have lost much of their former cachet.

Dress **£25–30** *Cardigan* **£65–75**

"The trick of wearing mink is to look as though you are wearing a cloth coat. The trick of wearing a cloth coat is to look as though you are wearing a mink."

► Made by Marguerite Rubel of San Francisco, this green velvet evening coat is typical of period styling. In contrast to slim, fitted suits and body-moulding dresses, coats were wide and boxy. Extravagantly large buttons were a popular feature as were decorative often asymmetric collars. Sleeves were three-quarter length, rendering the wearing of gloves a necessity in order to keep warm; further protection was provided by the pockets. Produced in jewel-coloured velvets, such coats still look fashionable today and are popular with collectors .

£70–80

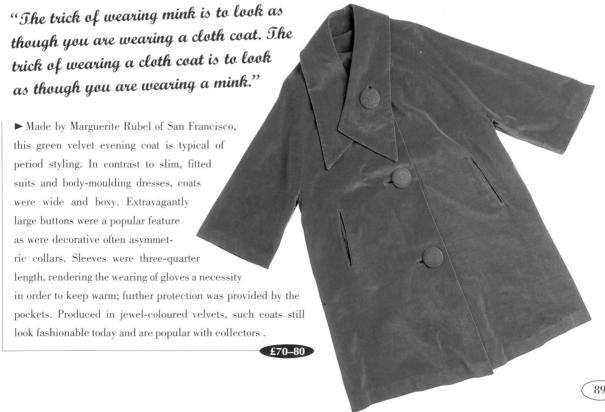

◀ The poodle was a popular motif in clothing as well as in the decorative arts. The felt poodle skirt is one of the fashion icons of the period, popular with young American girls in the 1950s and sought after today by rock 'n' roll enthusiasts. Good examples can be hard to find. This American skirt has two appliquéd poodles with diamanté collars linked together by a gold braid lead. It is shown with a cropped top decorated with a poodle bow.

Skirt **£150–200** *Top* **£24–27**

▶ A favourite option for summer throughout much of the decade was the New Look style cotton frock. This was tight at the waist with a slim-fitting bodice and full skirt, made fuller still by the addition of stiff petticoats. Skirts and dresses were bought off the peg or were often made up by hand. "You would buy the fabric during the week and run up a new skirt for a weekend party", recalls one 1950s teenager. Traditional textile manufacturers had to compete with the new synthetic wonder fabrics and developed high-quality, easy-care cottons. "Sunshine skirt fabrics – easy to make up for carefree weekends and holidays – quick to wash, drip dry and wear again because they are all Grafton 'Madrigal' Minimiron 'no-iron' cottons", boasted a typically cheerful period advertisement, offering brightly coloured prints. These two cotton printed dresses are typical of the period. The multicoloured dress in a bold, hand-painted abstract print is by Lo Roco and comes with a matching bolero jacket. The black and white dress is unlabelled and is shown with an elasticated cinch belt, a favourite accessory of the period.

'You would buy the fabric during the week and run up a new skirt for a weekend party.'

£15–35 *Each*

◀ Like furnishing fabrics, dress materials came in a huge variety of colourful patterns. Textile companies such as Horrockses employed talented artists and designers, and imaginative prints were produced by many other British companies. Skirts could be decorated with anything from flowers to street scenes – Paris, London and Venice being particularly popular. "They were clothes that looked happy", remembers one nostalgic wearer. "After rationing, and clothes made out of everything from hand-me-downs to blackout material, we all wanted a bit of colour." Both of these skirts are home-made. The pattern on the cream skirt is inspired by the opera. The black skirt is decorated with vegetables (including peppers), fruit, and straw-covered Chianti bottles. Such items can be very inexpensive today, but buyer beware. Women have grown over the decades and tend not to wear corsets. By today's standards, many 1950s clothes come in small to medium sizes.

£10–30 *Each*

"After rationing, and clothes made out of everything from hand-me-downs to blackout material, we all wanted a bit of colour."

▶ Highly decorative sequinned and painted skirts similar to this one were produced in Mexico. The Mexican influence was also expressed in the popularity of frilled, off-the-shoulder blouses and peasant-style cotton skirts. This black velvet skirt and top emblazoned with golden eagles appear to have been designed for the American market and it is unusual to find a matching set. Such items are very popular today. However, similar skirts continued to be made after the 1950s and it can be difficult to identify period examples.

Skirt **£65–95** *Top* **£25–35**

"Sunshine skirt fabrics"

91

▼ Whereas the New Look style remained popular for summer frocks, winter and spring suits were slimmer skirted and more tailored. This green tweed suit with a fake-fur collar was made by the British company Kelstree. It is shown together with a fake-fur hat. The post-war boom in man-made fibres brought a wealth of artificial animal skins onto the market. "No moths destroy, no weather wilts this magnificent coat of nylon simulation beaver", claimed an advertisement for Furleen. Suits from the 1950s tend to be well-made and lined.

Suit **£40–50** Hat **£20–25**

◄ ▲ The United States produced some of the smartest ready-to-wear garments of the decade. The yellow bouclé suit has a scarf collar and is made by Garland's St Louis, with a label inscribed: "That Devonbrook Look". The pink foil suit is by Saks Fifth Avenue. The late 1950s saw the fashion for colourful suits. "All the colours of the spectrum make daytime news in Paris", reported *Vogue* in 1958, noting also the "interesting necklines". Collars changed with every season. Magazines recommended using and making detach-able collars. "Be up to your ears in fashion," commanded *Woman's Own*; "knit the huge mohair collar decreed by Pierre Cardin!"

£70–90 Each

► Made in the United States and dating from the mid-1950s, this short, flared, pink woollen coat was known as a topper. Such coats were meant for springtime wear, and colours tended to be bright and light to set off the latest suits. "Striking ensembles... spring suits with that added something", noted a 1955 advertisement in *National Bellas Hess*, which was offering a topper for $7.98 or a topper with a "harmonizing" pink suit for $17.50.

£35–50

"they looked like bags of potatoes"

◄ The chemise, better known as the sack dress, arrived in 1957. Dior, Balenciaga and Givenchy all experimented with the waistless dress, which sharply divided opinion. Young girls brought sack dresses in their thousands. Older women were less convinced and some men claimed that "they looked like bags of potatoes". After Dior's death in 1957, his mantle was taken up by Yves St Laurent (b.1936). For his first collection in 1958 St Laurent launched the "Trapeze" dress. "Simply the most important and fully formulated line in Paris", gushed *Vogue*. "His wedge-shaped silhouette – called somewhat misleadingly the Trapeze line – is flared gently from narrow shoulders to a smooth wide hemline." This Trapeze-shaped green silk dress, bearing the label Marian Sue, shows the move toward loose-fitting, geometric lines that marked the end of the decade, heralded the end of the corsetted waist and the hourglass figure, and presaged the style of the 1960s.

£40–48

► If you couldn't afford a designer outfit, the answer was to make your own. These *Vogue* patterns date from the late 1950s to the early 1960s. They came complete with a *Vogue* label to sew onto the finished outfit and often still have swatches of fabric pinned to the packet. Covers can be very attractive and such patterns can still be found in charity shops and car boot sales.

Each **£5**

Casual Styles

The feminine fashions which had women teetering on spiky heels and wearing hats and gloves were countered by a more relaxed and casual look, particularly among the young. "She's 18 and she chooses trousers because somehow one always seems to end up sitting on the floor in her room", noted a fashion feature in *Vogue* (1952). Many women had worn trousers from necessity during World War II and they became increasingly fashionable in the 1950s. Ankle-length Capri pants and the shorter "pedal pushers" teamed with flat shoes were adopted by teenage girls, "though you would only ever wear them at weekends and for sporty occasions, never in town", remembers one London teenager. Even icons of femininity such as Marilyn Monroe and Princess Alexandra were photographed wearing jeans. As the decade passed, this casual look became more popular. There was a growing focus on teenage fashions derived from music and street style rather than haute couture houses which marked the end of the dominance of Paris and paved the way for the youth-oriented fashions of the 1960s.

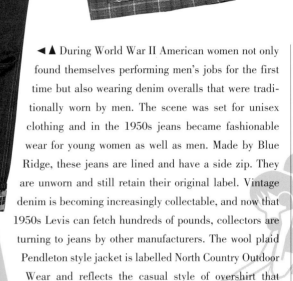

◄▲ During World War II American women not only found themselves performing men's jobs for the first time but also wearing denim overalls that were traditionally worn by men. The scene was set for unisex clothing and in the 1950s jeans became fashionable wear for young women as well as men. Made by Blue Ridge, these jeans are lined and have a side zip. They are unworn and still retain their original label. Vintage denim is becoming increasingly collectable, and now that 1950s Levis can fetch hundreds of pounds, collectors are turning to jeans by other manufacturers. The wool plaid Pendleton style jacket is labelled North Country Outdoor Wear and reflects the casual style of overshirt that would have accompanied jeans or trousers.

£20–25 *Each*

◄ Figure-hugging Capri or pirate pants became popular during the 1950s. They were tight fitting down to the ankle with a side or back zip because front fastenings were considered rather too suggestive for female wear. The trousers were worn with flat shoes and were often teamed with an off-the-shoulder blouse or a large sloppy-Joe sweater. Animal prints, the wilder the better, were the height of fashion. The leopardskin pattern makes these American Capri pants particularly desirable.

£25–30

▶ In the United Stated the Western look was worn by girls as well as boys. Cowboy programmes were hugely successful on television. Popular heroes such as Hopalong Cassidy and Roy Rogers were used to endorse children's clothing and toys as manufacturers became increasingly aware of television's ability to influence a new generation of young consumers. The label on this cowgirl outfit reads "Carole Sue by Shirly of Atlanta". Like the leather ranch boots, the outfit has never been worn and is in perfect condition.

Boots **£65–75** Suit **£40–50**

◀ The beaded cardigan was a favourite American accessory. The craze was popularized by Mainbocher (1891–1976), couturier to Wallis Simpson, who also designed cardigans for evening wear. These examples, like many from the period, were made in Hong Kong for the American market. Beading can be fragile and price depends on condition and the type of wool used (natural or man-made fibres).

£25–45

▶ It was not only the United States that stimulated the fashion for casual wear but also Italy. Emilio Pucci (1914–92), Florentine nobleman, bomber pilot and champion skier, became famous in the 1950s for his elegant casual separates. Pucci was known for tight-fitting trousers in jewelled shades and, above all, his brilliantly coloured, boldly patterned silk shirts. A Pucci shirt was a coveted status symbol in the 1950s and 1960s. As the price range below shows, they are equally sought after today. Because the patterns were loud, particularly in the psychedelic 1960s, shirts were often thrown away when fashions changed and original items are now hard to find. Photographed in 1954, this Audrey "Hepburnesque" model wears Capri pants and a Pucci Palio-print silk shirt.

£200–250

Lingerie and Swimwear

"Without foundations there can be no fashion", insisted Christian Dior. The look of the period was entirely dependent on corsetry. The 1950s was a golden age for manufacturers of sternly controlling underwear. Fashion magazines were filled with advertisements for waist nippers (also known as "waspies" or guêpières), girdles, and corselettes. Not since before World War I had women been so constricted by their undergarments, although companies were swift to point out the increased comfort provided by new man-made fibres. "You have been spared yesterday's agonies of whalebones and tight lacing", insisted an advertisement in 1951 for nylon rollover girdles. Whereas waists had to be pulled in, breasts had to point out, and what nature lacked, wiring and circle-stitching could provide. Vintage underwear might seem fascinating but who would want to buy it today? Some who dress in 1950s fashion go the whole way. "The clothes just don't look right without the proper garments underneath", claims one enthusiast. According to dealers, these ultra-feminine items are also popular with male customers.

◄ The "sweater girl" fashion started in the 1940s and was most famously embodied by Lana Turner, who helped stimulate demand for the pointed circle-stitch bra. An advertisement for circle-stitch bras promised: "Nylon adjustable band under each cup assures uplift from underneath... lifts and separates each breast by itself; does away with droop and sagging to the side; puts you way out in front!" The white bra featured here is a Miss Youthflex Whirl by Miss America. The black satin circle-stitch bra is labelled "Exquisite Form".

£20–24

▼ During World War II stockings were virtually unobtainable. Women were reduced to wearing ankle socks or using leg make-up with a line drawn up the back of each leg for the seams. Nylon stockings which came from the United States were hugely coveted. "My first pair were sent to me after the war by a sailor stationed in Bermuda, I was the envy of every girl in Bushey", recalls a former English teenager. By the early 1950s stockings were more readily available. "A refreshing change has taken place in the last twelve months from the gentle craft of finding nylons to the subtle art of choosing them", noted an advertisement in *Vogue* (1952). These American stockings dating from the 1950s are still in their original packaging. Seamed stockings are more popular with enthusiasts today than the seamless "barelegged" look that appeared in the late 1950s.

—— *Seamed* **£10–15**

—— *Unseamed* **£5**

◄While body-hugging knitwear required a well-controlled chest, the fashion for neat little tailored suits required a correspondingly neat little body. "For trumpet skirts, sheath skirts and all their near relations, hips must be unobtrusive. The long unbroken line from waist to knee allows no ugly bulges, provides no camouflage for unsightly rolls", warned *Vogue* in 1951. Advertisements stressed that girdles would soon put a girl into shape, "the shape that controls your future...". These period examples include a nylon leopardskin panty girdle by Vanity Fair; a white satin boned roll-on girdle; and a striped "floating contour" girdle by Nestleform. Value today is largely dependent on the perceived sex-appeal of the item.

White satin **£28–32**　*Leopardskin* **£38–42**　*Striped* **£13–15**

"firm underbust wiring"

◄ Home of new technology, the United States led the production of corsetry and underwear. In Britain *Vogue* noted that "fabulous corsets create the fabulous figures of American women", and that the fashion for backless evening dresses necessitated "firm underbust wiring" for a "safe décolleté look". These boned, strapless all-in-one corselettes are both American. The white lace model is labelled Adonna and the black padded corselette is called Lady Marlene.

£35–45 *Each*

► The wide skirted New Look was supported by layers of frilly nylon petticoats. "A full skirt without a stiff petticoat can't help looking limp and far too long", warned *Woman* magazine in July 1956. Also known as can-can petticoats, these were popular throughout the decade. An American mail order catalogue advertised "Flirty Nylon Poufs – New Paris Shapes! New Paris Colours!" as late as 1959. Petticoats came in a rainbow of colours and were worn two or more at a time. In order to keep them crisp, they would often be dipped in sugar solution and drip dried. This petticoat dates from the 1950s, but similar examples are still being produced today.

£38–42

◄This is probably the most curious item featured in this book. Familiarly known as "a bum enhancer", it is a pair of nylon pants with rounded foam rubber pads fitted into the lining. According to a 1950s American mail order catalogue, this "secret helper" provides "that perfect uplift for unrivalled curves, along with centre separation for that natural look". Other versions also offered padding for the hips as well as the behind. "Feels Real!", assured the advertisements. "Bum enhancers" are again being produced today and are apparently popular in Japan.

£20–25

"Feels Real!"

► Dating from the 1950s, this white lace, backless bra is shown together with a pair of white lace, "baby doll" waist-cinch pants. Heavily boned, these waist-whittling pants are cruelly constricting, hence perhaps their appeal to certain collectors today. The American 1950s pin-up and bondage star Betty Page was photographed wearing identical underwear, and like other items from the period, her erotic photographic legacy is currently fashionable and enjoying cult status.

Bra **£12–15** *Pants* **£38–42**

◄Nylon was easily washable and stimulated the use of bright colours as well as pastel shades. This collection of multicoloured nylon knickers dates from the mid-1950s. Each pair is embroidered with a day of the week. They have never been worn and are still contained in their original, satin-quilted presentation box.

£30–36

◄ Nylon was a popular choice for self-consciously glamorous and colourful negligée sets, such as this American example. Because artificial fibres were still comparatively new, manufacturers were careful to give precise washing instructions. "This beautiful garment is made to exacting standards by Rogers. Care for it properly and it will give you long and lovely service", reads the tag on this unworn garment. An alternative to this long look was the extremely short "baby doll" night-dress, popularized by the eponymous 1956 film starring Carol Baker as a child bride. Many women had taken to wearing pyjamas during World War II, and these remained popular throughout the 1950s, often with a mandarin or rounded Peter Pan collar.

£35–45

▶ These American bathing costumes date from the 1950s. The new synthetic fabrics were perfect for quick-drying, body-hugging swimwear. Many swimsuits concealed bones and padding, maintaining "the figure flattering precision of a corset and a brassiere". An alternative to this structured look was the two-piece bathing suit in bright cotton, with romper style or skirted bottom. This little girl style was inspired by wartime shortages when the government stipulated that the material used in swimwear should be reduced by ten percent. "The saving has been effected – in the region of the midriff", reported the *New York Times* dryly. In 1946, French designer Louis Reard launched the bikini, named after Bikini Atoll where the United States had just detonated the atomic bomb. As the press reported, the bikini used less than one square foot of fabric and "revealed everything about a girl except her mother's maiden name". Until the late 1950s, however, the majority of two-pieces maintained comparatively generous proportions.

£20–30 *Each*

Hats and Scarves

Hats were still *de rigueur* for formal daywear during the 1950s. "I would never have dreamt of shopping in Knightsbridge without wearing a smart hat, white gloves and full make-up", recalls a former English model from the period. Hats tended either to be very large or very small, fashions veering from flying-saucer shaped coolie hats to the tiniest delicate flowered *toques*. Paris couturiers launched new designs every season but, by the end of the decade, the taste for more casual clothes and bouffant hairstyles signalled the end of the hat as an everyday necessity. Headscarves became popular during World War II when women working in munitions factories wrapped their heads up turban-style to protect their hair. The headscarf became a favourite British accessory, most famously modelled by the Queen. Highly inventive designs both in hats and scarves were produced during the 1950s and good quality examples are sought after. With hats condition can be a problem, although steaming can help to restore a crushed model to its former glory.

▲ "The prettiest summer for years, no hint of austere chic; it is smart to be frankly charming – a hat may be no more than one swirled chiffon flower, a chignon cap of wild rose blossoms", claimed *Vogue* in June, 1954. Tiny "half hats" shaped like flowers were very popular in the first half of the 1950s. The pink hat is made from bouclé felt with a rose printed interior. The navy-blue hat by Bes Ben of Chicago is shaped out of beaded, plastic flowers and shows how synthetic materials were considered acceptable for the most formal garments.

Navy-blue hat **£35–45**   *Pink hat* **£25–30**

▼ This straw hat is made by Greenland's Limited, Hereford, England, and is in immaculate condition. The flat-crowned, wide-brimmed hat was a favourite 1950s shape; its circular line provided a perfect balance to the New Look skirt. Popular designs in straw included the coolie hat, made by Balenciaga and copied by every high street milliner, and the chic French schoolgirl hat with an upturned brim, a look inspired by the gamine Leslie Caron in the film *Gigi*.

£10–15

► Turbans were popular during World War II and throughout the following decade, one of their most celebrated creators being the Parisian milliner, Paulette. This selection shows the variety of colours and material available. The pink straw turban is made by Christian Dior; it is finely pleated and precisely modelled. The green jersey turban is more commonplace and has no maker's name; the turban covered with artificial flowers is by the American company, B.Altman & Co.

Green & Flower turban **£10–15** *Pink turban* **£30–35**

◄These silk scarves are by the British manufacturer Jacqmar. One commemorates the Coronation of Queen Elizabeth (1953), the other shows a romantic *fin de siècle* Paris street scene. The Coronation inspired a huge variety of scarves, ranging from comparatively expensive, elegant designs (such as this example) to inexpensive rayon scarves decorated with patriotic verses and unflattering portraits of the Royal family. Prices vary according to quality.

Coronation scarf **£40–60** *Paris scarf* **£30–50**

"Hats of Distinction"

► Small, ladylike hats provided the natural complement to slimline, elegant suits. The black straw hat with a single feather secured by a jet bead is labelled "Eva Mae – Hats of Distinction". Small loops on either side enable the hat to be pinned or secured with elastic to the head. The check hat with two wings of cockerel feathers is unlabelled and is kept in place by combs.

£30–40 *Each*

Handbags and Shoes

The 1950s was a golden age for handbag design. New materials spawned fanciful fashions, epitomized by the Lucite handbag. A by-product of wartime technology, these American perspex creations were fun, modern, and bought by everyone from teenage girls to dowagers. Period prices began at a couple of dollars but today, these charming, if impractical box-bags are highly collectable.

The New Look that shaped fashion and drew attention to the ankles also affected shoe design. Whilst "flatties" were fine for casual wear, more formal clothes required heels and the 1950s saw the introduction of the stiletto. "I don't know who invented the high heel, but all women owe him a lot", claimed Marilyn Monroe, whose famous wiggle was supposedly contrived by having one heel slightly shorter than the other. By the mid-1950s wooden stilettos, which were easily broken, were replaced by plastic-covered metal heels, resulting in a vertiginous spike that pierced floors across the world, causing stilettos to be banned from public buildings. This sharp heel was matched by a winkle-picker toe, so narrow that by the end of the decade women were buying shoes two sizes too large in order to fit into them.

▲ Shoe design occasionally verged on the surreal. These unusual and rare "invisible stilettos" date from the late 1950s; the high heel has been replaced by a metal sole extension. Like many other innovative designs of the period, they came from Italy. Perhaps unsurprisingly the style did not catch on.

£100–150

▲ The 1950s clear vinyl clutch bag (right) and the carved Lucite bag are both decorated with rhinestones. The American Springolator mules have vinyl tops and perspex heels. Celebrated Italian shoe designer Salvatore Ferragamo (1898–1960), credited with inventing the platform sole, the wedge heel and the stiletto heel, stunned the fashion world in 1947 with a transparent nylon sandal that made the foot look daringly naked, launching the craze for clear plastic, fantasy footwear.

Handbag **£50–60** *Mules* **£65–70** *Clutch bag* **£25–30**

► These plastic handbags summon up the whimsical spirit of the 1950s and their popularity almost exactly spans the decade. The beehive handbag (far right) was produced by New York manufacturer Llewellyn in 1951, although other firms did copy this design. The honey-coloured, beehive base is surmounted by a carved top, set with gilded metal bees. The black plastic handbag (right), with double handles and large brilliants, is another Llewellyn design and also came in clear plastic. Bags sometimes retain their original labels or a maker's mark – the major companies include Llewellyn, Rialto, Willardy, Florida Handbags and Patricia of Miami.

— *Black bag* **£140–180** *Beehive bag* **£150–200**

▼ High heeled mules (backless slippers), were popular in the 1950s. Dior's shoemaker Roger Vivier (b.1913) created some elegant examples for evening wear, and Marilyn Monroe sported a pair of fluffy mules in the 1955 comedy *The Seven Year Itch*. Feminine to the point of mincing, mules are often associated with the image of the dumb blonde. They were certainly designed for fun, rather than serious physical activity, as implied by the maker's name on the red example (left)," Folly of California".

£23–25

"Folly of California"

► In the mid-1950s, raffia and wicker baskets decorated with artificial fruit were popular for spring and summer. The white wicker picnic-box handbag is decorated with plastic apples; the inner label reads: "Especially for you by Las Doradas". The circular handbag is made from plasticized raffia and is decorated with colourful glass beads, and the ubiquitous poodle motif.

— *Picnic bag* **£85–95** *Poodle bag* **£65–85**

◄Rare animal skins were popular for handbags and shoes, reflecting the post-war craze for exotic decoration, which expressed itself in every medium. Lizards, alligators, snakes and crocodiles were slaughtered for their decorative and water-resistant skins. A crocodile handbag was a status symbol and some examples were decorated with the claws, head, or even the complete taxidermed corpse of a baby alligator, a fashionable trope that appears horrifying today. The handbag featured here is made from lizard skin; the high stiletto shoes with brass toe taps are snakeskin and marked "Daphne Taylor: Genuine Cobra". They are shown together with a nylon leopardskin print scarf, a popular 1950s accessory.

Handbag **£38–42** *Shoes* **£65–75** *Scarf* **£10–15**

► Beaded handbags were a fashionable accessory in the 1940s and 1950s. Designs ranged from traditional floral patterns to abstract shapes, and from silhouettes to complete all-over beading, also known as caviar beading. All of these handbags are American. The black velvet handbag, labelled "Souré New York", is decorated with beaded spiders' webs. The multicoloured handbag is made of printed cotton and is covered with clear glass beads. On the white silk handbag the beaded design is protected by a layer of shiny clear vinyl. Pale coloured handbags were often similarly encased, but as soon as plastic became associated with being inexpensive and nasty rather than new and stylish, the fashion for these coverings decreased.

Black velvet bag **£85–95**

Multi-coloured bag **£45–55** *White bag* **£55–65**

►This bouclé tube handbag, also known as a sausage bag, dates from the 1950s and is shown with a red and black brocade bag made by Myers, USA. Although gloves were not as popular in the 1950s as before World War II (other than for seasonal necessity), they were still worn for more formal occasions: long gloves made from leather or fabric for the evening and wrist or three-quarter-length gloves for daytime wear. Engraved with the Festival of Britain insignia, the gilt metal device is a glove holder, designed so that when a lady took off her gloves, she could then attach them to her handbag.

Glove holder **£10–15**

Handbags each **£35–45** *Gloves* **£15–20**

▼ Imaginative handbag designs are extremely sought after today. This white leather handbag by Anne Marie of Paris is shaped like fanned-out playing cards (one of the favourite motifs of the period) and the clasp is a pair of gilded dice. Shown alongside are two pairs of American golden shoes. Gold was a favourite colour for eveningwear and Salvatore Ferragamo went as far as making a pair of sandals out of 18 carat gold. The mules are called Qualicraft Casualets and have a moulded plywood base with steel stiletto heels. The golden-soled slippers are lined in pink silk and were designed by Taj Tajerie in the late 1950s. They have a turned-up toe and an unusual central heel with a triangular tip. Hollywood star, Gloria Swanson, famous for her glamorous wardrobe, owned several pairs of these shoes.

Shoes **£50–60**

Handbag **£200–250**

Mules **£40–45**

Cosmetics and Perfume

Cosmetic production ground to a halt during World War II. "Cosmetics are as essential to a woman as a reasonable supply of tobacco is to a man," argued *Vogue*. "Only when a woman looks her best can she feel and do her best." With the return of peace and ladylike fashions, the industry boomed. Manufacturers produced cosmetics of ever increasing luxury with ingredients ranging from human placenta to pulverized pearls. New styles emerged. The 1950s saw the introduction of the exotic "doe-eyed" look, with eyes lined with pencil and swept into almond shapes and lashes darkened with mascara below plucked and pencilled eyebrows. Detractors likened it to the bride of Frankenstein. Complexions were pale and perfect, sponged with foundation and pressed with powder, constrasting with glossy lips. Magazines stressed the importance of immaculate grooming at all times and women had no compunction about fixing their faces in public. "They take out boxes between courses and put them on the table", complained Coco Chanel. "How can one be elegant doing that?" Nevertheless, compacts appeared in every lady's handbag.

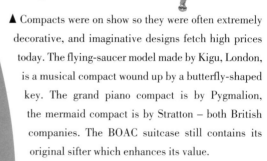

▲ Compacts were on show so they were often extremely decorative, and imaginative designs fetch high prices today. The flying-saucer model made by Kigu, London, is a musical compact wound up by a butterfly-shaped key. The grand piano compact is by Pygmalion, the mermaid compact is by Stratton – both British companies. The BOAC suitcase still contains its original sifter which enhances its value.

Flying saucer **£200–250** *Mermaid* **£35–45**
Grand piano **£95–125** *Suitcase* **£75–85**

▼ Designed as a wedding gift, the compact decorated with a black cat was made in England. The compact with a marcasite poodle is by Stratton. "Good Taste–Good Gift – the only compact with the self-opening inner lid", promised an advertisement in 1954. The perfumes held by black velour cats are Primitif and Hypnotique by Max Factor and have plastic covers (not shown). In the centre is a poodle soap.

Poodle compact **£75–85** *Cat compact* **£35–45**
Perfumes **£15–25**
Soap **£10–20**

► Around The Clock perfume (far right) by Stuart Products, St Paul, Minnesota, USA, came in a plastic container shaped like a grandfather clock. When the perfume was finished, the circular bottle could be removed and the case could serve as a holder for a fob watch. In the 1950s Schiaparelli, the couturier, decorated scent boxes with musical notes, a favourite 1950s image. They appear here on a less expensive perfume called Heartbeat by Leigh Perfumers, Shulton Inc., USA. *A Bientot* by Lentheric shows similar multi-coloured graphics typical of period style. The spotted parasol is a novelty perfume bottle that was designed for the handbag.

A Bientot £45–55   *Spotted parasol* £85–95

Heartbeat £45–55   *Around The Clock* £65–75

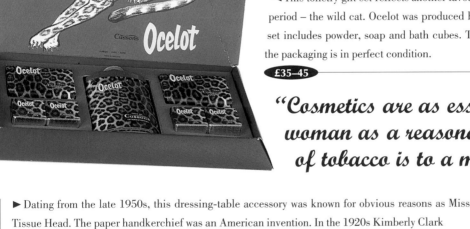

◄ This toiletry gift set reflects another favourite animal motif of the period – the wild cat. Ocelot was produced by Cussons and this gift set includes powder, soap and bath cubes. They are all unused and the packaging is in perfect condition.

£35–45

"Cosmetics are as essential to a woman as a reasonable supply of tobacco is to a man."

► Dating from the late 1950s, this dressing-table accessory was known for obvious reasons as Miss Tissue Head. The paper handkerchief was an American invention. In the 1920s Kimberly Clark brought out Kleenex as make-up removers (hence their name); however, they soon realized their potential as handkerchiefs. "Use Kleenex in place of germ-carrying handkerchiefs", stressed the advertisements. Although they came in "handy pull-out boxes", a more decorative alternative was often preferred. With their plasticized faces and nylon hair these tissue containers might not be the ultimate in elegance but they are certainly rich in kitsch appeal.

£20–25 *Each*

Costume Jewellery

"Diamonds are a girl's best friend", sang Marilyn Monroe in *Gentlemen Prefer Blondes* in 1955. It was pretend not precious stones that adorned the stars of Hollywood films, and it was the influence of the movies that helped popularize paste. In the United States in the 1950s costume jewellery was worn by everybody from teenage girls buying plastic poppet beads at five-and-dime stores to the First Lady herself. For President Eisenhower's Inauguration ball in 1953, Mamie Eisenhower wore a pink dress sewn with 2,000 rhinestones and a choker of faux pearls by Trifari. "I love costume jewellery", she assured those who questioned her unprecedented "fake" choice. The United States produced some of the finest costume jewellers of the decade. In Europe, the field was led by the great couturiers who designed fashion pieces to go with their collections. Today these fabulous fakes have become very collectable. The best designer examples fetch high prices and tend to be signed, often on the back or clasp. At the other end of the market, mass-produced fun jewellery from the 1950s can still be bought for very little expense.

◄ These lovely bird brooches and the diamanté grapes pin and earrings were made by Trifari in the 1950s. "Every exquisite piece designed by Trifari is a triumph in the art of costume jewellery", claimed an advertisement in 1946 for the very successful Rhode Island company. Trifari was founded in 1918 by Gustavo Trifari and Leo F.Krussman. In 1930 designer Alfred Philippe, who had created precious jewellery for Cartier, and Van Cleef and Arpels, joined the team. Trifari became widely known for their imaginative high-quality costume jewellery. They provided the jewellery for many famous Broadway productions as well as paste for Mamie Eisenhower.

Diamanté set **£85–95** *Brooches* **£25–30**

◄ New York designer Miriam Haskell (1899–1981) was one of the most popular jewellery designers of her generation and remains so with today's collectors. "I want my jewellery to be as unusual and ravishing as the women who wear it, for there to be nothing like it", she claimed. Haskell was particularly known for her luscious pearls which gained their distinctive lustre from being dipped in fish scales. This gilt brass, pearl and crystal Miriam Haskell necklace with matching earrings dates from the 1950s.

£300–350

► Copper jewellery was a particular fad of the 1950s. Renoir of California was founded by designer Jerry Fels. The company produced plain copper pieces such as this necklace, bracelet and earrings set. Matisse Limited, the sister company established in 1952, used copper decorated with brightly coloured enamels, as shown here in the palette brooch and earrings. As the names suggest, Renoir/Matisse created self-consciously artistic pieces with hand-crafted appeal. Designs were inspired by abstract imagery and amoebic forms. Copper jewellery could be worn with both formal and more casual wear and provided a modern contrast to the more traditional paste and pearls.

Palette brooch & earrings **£70–90** *Bracelet, necklace & earrings* **£50–60**

"I want my jewellery to be as unusual and ravishing as the women who wear it, for there to be nothing like it."

◄ In the 1950s daytime suits were set off with large brooches pinned to the lapel. This King of Hearts brooch is by Kramer of New York, founded in 1943 by Louis Kramer, the firm responsible for making Dior's jewellery in the United States.

£50–60

► These heart- and moon-shaped brooches were produced by the American costume jewellers, Weiss. Established by Albert Weiss in 1942, the company was known for its high quality rhinestones. Crystal was often imported from the Rhineland area of Germany, hence the term rhinestone.

£40–50 *Each*

◀This collection of sunglasses dates from the 1950s. The more extravagant the design the higher the price. The batwing frames (bottom left) represent 1950s styling at its most confidently outrageous and are correspondingly more expensive than the less flamboyant styles.

Batwing frames **£85–95** *Others* **£10–20**

▶During the 1950s, costume jewellery could be imaginative and above all fun. Both of these pieces are unsigned and inspired by champagne. The earrings are miniature ice buckets covered in leatherette and they contain tiny plastic bottles. The gilt metal bracelet has a distinctive charm – a diamanté champagne glass brimming with bubbly champagne made from pearls. Pendant and charm bracelets were extremely popular during the period. They were worn by teenagers and, famously, by Mamie Eisenhower, whose bracelet, clanking with charms representing achievements in her husband's presidential career, became one of her fashion trademarks.

Earrings **£55–65** *Bracelet* **£55–65**

◀This large pearl and diamanté brooch is by Christian Dior. Costume jewellery increased in popularity along with ready-to-wear clothes. Only a tiny minority of women could afford individually tailored, *haute couture* fashions, and during the 1950s Dior and other designers began experimenting with *pret-à-porter* lines and decorative accessories so as to increase their market share and their profits. The ever practical Coco Chanel was one of the first to create fashion jewellery, modelling her creations on her own real gems so that, she claimed, women could look like a fortune without having to spend one. Dior's jewellery designs were produced in the United States by Kramer of New York and in West Germany by Grosse and Mayer.

£125–150

►In the 1940s and 1950s even the most eminent costume jewellers used plastic. The American company Trifari, for example, produced a series of animal and insect brooches with clear Lucite bodies known as "jelly bellies" which are highly collectable today. Plastic also led to the proliferation of cheap and cheerful novelty jewellery, designed for fun and available for literally pence. These American earrings from the 1950s are old stock and still in their original packaging. In the centre is a plastic poppet-bead necklace. Necklaces like this were popular with teenage girls. They were worn several strands at a time and teamed with baggy sweater and slim-line trousers for a casual look.

£5 *Each*

◄ Animal motifs were a traditional favourite for jewellery and none more so than the image of the cat. These brooches date from the 1950s – the copper brooch is signed Barkin, the rhinestone cat with a diamond in the tip of its tail is by Warner.

Rhinestone brooch **£25–35**
Copper brooch **£25–35**

Menswear

For the majority of men suits were normal wear during the 1950s. "Whether you were a city gent or a teddy boy you had to look smart", remembers one London taxi driver. At the beginning of the decade, American styles were fashionable: single-breasted suits, wide trousers with high turn-ups, polished brogues and a loud tie. This look was later supplanted by the Italian suit: short "bum-freezer" Roman jackets, narrow trousers without cuffs, slim tie and winklepicker shoes, a prototype of 1960s "Mod" style. An expanding economy and increased leisure time stimulated demand for sportswear. The United States pioneered colourful casual clothes for men and led the way in teenage fashion. Beatniks (like the Paris existentialists) popularized anti-establishment, scruffy dress: large sweaters, crumpled cords and duffel coats. Rebel heroes from James Dean to Elvis Presley strutted in jeans, T-shirts and leather jackets, transforming working clothes into a street style that has never gone out of fashion.

◄After the austerity of wartime, men, like women, were eager for colour. Wide ties, hand-painted with everything from flowers to dancing girls, became extremely popular. In the United States there were tie collecting clubs and enthusiasts owned literally thousands of examples. In Britain, Cecil Gee was the first to import the American look to his London shop in 1946. "After the blitz, here comes the Ritz", he promised, and on Saturday mornings queues of men lined up to buy American suits and loud "scrambled egg" ties. Considered flash, verging on the disreputable, such ties are sought after today.

£15–35 *Each*

◄This American suit is single breasted with two buttons, it has turn-ups on the trousers and a slight blue fleck in the material. This style was popular in the first half of the 1950s. Suits were not only the uniform of corporate man in the United States but also popular with students of select East Coast universities – the Ivy Leaguers. The Ivy League look also became fashionable in England during the 1950s, when an American suit was a coveted status symbol. This suit is shown with a blue gabardine shirt and hand-painted silk tie, both dating from the same period. Suits were often worn till they fell apart and examples in good condition are hard to find.

Suit **£85–95**

Shirt **£24–28**

Tie **£15–25**

►▼ Gabardine, a hardwearing tightly woven fabric, was much used for men's leisurewear during the 1950s. These colourful casual "gab" jackets are highly sought after. The red and black example is reversible. Known as a "weekender", the other jacket is the height of desirability. Pink and black are favourite colours with collectors, especially when combined with a diamond or argyle pattern. Such jackets are rare, especially in good condition, hence the high price.

Below **£800–1000** *Right* **£150–200**

►To the bemused horror of many adults, the 1950s saw the emergence of rebellious teenage gangs, ranging from leather-jacketed bikers in the United States to teddy boys in Britain. The teddy boys took their name from Edward VII and their look fused Edwardian opulence with American glamour. Long draped jackets were worn with brightly coloured, flashy waistcoats and bootlace, cowboy ties. Short drain-pipe trousers showed off luminous socks and suede shoes with thick crepe soles known as "brothel creepers". City businessmen of the period had also adopted new "Edwardian" fashions: bowler hat, rolled up umbrella, three-piece suit and single breasted overcoat trimmed with a velvet collar. Teddy boys however, transformed this look into working-class style.

Teddy boy suit **£100–200**

◄ Traditionally worn by miners, cowboys and all those involved in hard manual labour, denim was transformed in the 1950s from everyday workwear into the fashionable uniform of rebellious youth. The famously "overpaid and over-sexed" GIs gave Europe its first glimpse of blue denim, and like nylons and chewing gum, a pair of American jeans was a glamorous and exotic status symbol. Denim jeans were modelled by every teenage hero from James Dean to Elvis Presley, whose films today inspire paroxysms of lust in vintage denim collectors. This Levi Strauss & Co. 507 XX jacket was designed in 1953. It has two breast pockets and is known as Levi's "Number Two" or "Second Edition" jacket. These Levi jeans also date from the 1950s. They are known as Capital Es, after the upper case E on the red Levi's tab on the pocket. (Since 1971 the company have spelt their name on the tab with a lower case e.) Vintage denim is highly desirable and because most old jeans tended, logically enough, to be thrown away, period examples are rare (especially in good condition) and correspondingly highly priced today. Enthusiasts wear these jeans turned up at the bottom to reveal the selvages; the white seams on the inside leg are another vintage feature.

Jacket **£700–750** *Jeans* **£700–750**

► A perfect combination with a pair of jeans was a leather jacket. This look was most famously embodied by Marlon Brando in *The Wild One* (1954) in which he wore heavy boots, turned-up jeans and a black leather biker's jacket – the epitome of lawless youth and the besuited adult's nightmare. The American blouson style jacket illustrated here is made by Campus and dates from the same period. It is brown horsehide, fully lined and extremely heavy.

£100–150

◄Western clothing was very popular during the 1950s and remains so with collectors today. The romance of the cowboy look combines the butch with the decorative and attracts legions of admirers both in the United States and across the world. The blue gabardine western trousers have a pocket in the shape of a pistol. The black and grey western shirt with floral embroidery and mother of pearl poppers is by H Bar C, California Ranchwear, a much sought after label.

Trousers **£55–65**

Jacket **£65–75**

► This selection of shoes from the 1950s are all old stock and unworn. Short black Harley Davidson boots were worn by Elvis Presley in the 1958 film, *King Creole*, starring Elvis as a night club singer dragged into the criminal underworld. The biker's boot, like jeans and leather jackets, became associated with teenage rebellion. They were worn by motor cycle gangs and modelled by James Dean in *Rebel Without A Cause* and Marlon Brando in *The Wild One*. The white buckskin lace-ups and loafers represent a less aggressive style. The slip-on shoe was a popular part of Ivy League dress and was known as a "penny loafer" from the custom of slipping a shiny cent into the cut out flap at the front. These shoes are all unworn.

Shoes **£75–85**

Boots **£180–210**

The popularity of ten pin bowling intensified in the United States in the 1950s. In 1953 the Golden Jubilee Tournament of the American Bowling Congress attracted 8,180 teams, an entry of over 41,000 people. In 1958 the Professional Bowlers Association was founded. This 1950s bowling shirt is made by Angeltown, California. Shirts came in a huge variety of colours and were customized with the title and symbol of the team on the back and the player's name on the front. Certain labels, including Angeltown and King Louis, are more desirable than others. Gabardine shirts are preferred to cotton shirts and price is also affected by the embroidery: the more detailed the image, the higher the price.

£32–42

▶The 1950s saw men adopting more colourful clothes. "I must protest against this 'brighter clothes for men' campaign", complained a female correspondent to *Woman* magazine in May 1953. "I've endured a journey sitting opposite a man in a bright blue suit, a pink shirt, flowing yellow and green tie, and striped yellow socks... what's the use of girls wearing colourful dresses if our men friends are going to put us in the shade?" Although effects were felt even in austere Britain, it was America that pioneered the fashion for multicoloured leisurewear, taking full advantage of the new synthetic materials and "miracle" drip-dry, non-crease fabrics that came into vogue after World War II. Known as a Hollywood shirt, this black and yellow rayon shirt with its loud pattern of flags and pennants dates from the late 1940s to the early 1950s. It has a long pointed collar, shoulder pads (designed to give an impression of breadth and height) and was made by Royal Palm, Miami. The snowflakes shirt (mid- to late 1950s) has a smaller collar and was manufactured by Van Heusen, USA. It is a cotton and rayon mix gabardine. Although the pattern is good, the brown colour is less desirable than other colours.

Yellow & black shirt £100–150 Brown shirt £75–100

◄▲ Hawaiian shirts were extremely fashionable in the 1940s and 1950s, their brilliant patterns and bright colours providing an exotic contrast to the utilitarian dullness of wartime uniform. The post-war period saw sportswear, even beach clothing, becoming more acceptable for casual dress. Shirts were mass-produced with roller-printed patterns in Japan and the United States as well as being manufactured in Hawaii. The Hawaiian shirt was worn by everyone from President Eisenhower to rock singers and film stars. Montgomery Clift, Burt Lancaster and Frank Sinatra all sported shirts made by the Cisco Company in the 1953 film *From Here To Eternity*. Collecting Hawaiian shirts has become a specialist field and many factors affect value. The most desirable examples tend to be those produced in Hawaii that are hand-sewn, hand-printed and finely illustrated. Certain mainland American labels are also popular. Shirts were produced in rayon, cotton and silk, and a sign of quality is pockets that match the pattern of the fabric. Condition is important (some dyes are prone to fading), as is the presence of a label which helps to identify the name and place of manufacture. Price is also affected by the complexity and rarity of the image. The brown and orange cotton shirt is from the late 1950s and was made in Hawaii by Ui Maikai. The turquoise shirt is unlabelled, rayon, and a mass-produced chainstore example. Shirts were teamed with matching shorts; these examples are from the 1950s.

Brown & orange shirt **£75–125** *Turquoise shirt* **£35–45** *Shorts* **£25–50**

After the horrors of World

War II there was a growing emphasis on the

young. In Britain free school milk and better health care and

nutrition, meant that children were bigger than ever before, and between

1946 and 1955 the infant death rate halved. Stronger and more numerous, children

also became psychologically more important. Dr Spock's Common Sense Book of Baby and

Childcare *(USA, 1946) sold millions of copies and influenced a whole generation of parents by*

counselling understanding rather than punishment, and stressing the individual needs of each child.

Leisure

The 1950s saw the birth of the teenager and the widening of the generation gap. Young people became an

independent force. Jobs and shorter working hours gave them money to spend and time to enjoy it.

They had their own clubs and coffee bars, their own fashions and music. A new breed of rebel

idols, from James Dean to Elvis Presley to Jack Kerouac, expressed their alienation from

the adult world and their desire to shake and rattle the establishment. This

final section celebrates fun and leisure in the 1950s: the emergence

of new toys, the birth of rock 'n' roll, and changing

trends in film and literature.

Toys

The post-World War II baby boom created a new generation of tiny consumers and a surge in demand for toys. The combination of new health and hygiene regulations and developing technologies changed manufacture. Model cars came with plastic windows and suspension, cheap vinyl dolls were mass-produced in their millions, and advertisements showed synthetic teddies being washed in machines and wrung through mangles. The development of children's television in the 1950s – *Watch with Mother* in Britain, *Disneyland* in America – introduced a range of juvenile heroes, from Muffin the Mule to Davy Crocket, and limitless marketing opportunities, from character puppets to furry-tailed hats. "Never underestimate the buying power of a child under seven" was the message aimed at advertisers in the 1950s. For boys, the influence of comics and science fiction resulted in new toys based on space age characters such as Dan Dare and the lantern-jawed Captain America, the grandfathers of the current generation of super-heroes. For girls, the decade drew to a close with the birth in 1959 of Barbie, the first teenage fashion doll. Produced by Mattel, Barbie had everything a pre-pubescent girl could wish for – breasts, long legs and a designer wardrobe.

◄ This plastic, walking, flirty-eyed doll, in her original cotton sundress, was made in the 1950s by British manufacturers Pedigree. The use of vinyl meant that wigs and moulded hair could be replaced by realistic tresses rooted into the doll's head. One of the attractions of this model was that little girls could wash the doll's hair without damaging the doll.

£80–85

▼ During World War II the British company Merrythought halted teddy bear manufacture to provide fleecy linings for helmets. After the war production resumed. Known as Cheeky, this popular bear was introduced in 1957. Its design differed from traditional models; the ears were extremely large and contained a bell, the eyes were plastic and the fabric synthetic. The bear is identifiable by the label stitched to the footpad and its distinctive squashed face and "cheeky" expression.

£300–400

► In 1949, engineer and amateur magician, Harry Corbett created Sooty from a teddy bear bought while on holiday in Blackpool. Three years later the whispering Sooty, and his squeaky friend Sweep the dog, made their first appearance on British television. The Sooty show was a huge hit. Today it is hosted by Harry's son Matthew Corbett and is Britain's longest running children's television programme. A wide range of "Sootiana" was produced in the 1950s, examples shown here include a Sooty xylophone and a rubber toy by Combex.

Rubber Sooty **£15–25** *Xylophone* **£10–15**

"Sootiana"

▼ Muffin the Mule first appeared on British television in 1951 and this heavy diecast puppet, manufactured by Lesney, was among the first licensed British toys to be based on a television character. This particular example has been loved and played with a great deal and is somewhat battered. Boxed and in good condition its value would be tripled.

£20–30

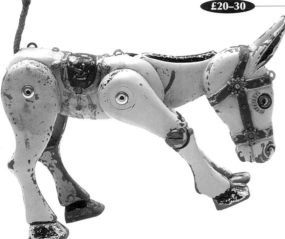

▼ It was not just the adult population who were involved with building new homes after the war. This Bayco Building Set by Plimpton dates from 1950s and was one of a number of popular toys which allowed children to create their own houses. However, the most significant construction kit to be developed during the period was Lego. Like other classic 1950s designs, Lego was Scandinavian and was launched in 1955 by the Danish firm founded by Ole Kirk Christiansen.

£40–50

◄ In the 1950s many toys were inspired by films, comics and science fiction. This Space Pilot 3 Colour Supersonic Gun and the Dan Dare Radio Station were both made by Merit. Dan Dare – "Pilot of the future" and hero of the *Eagle* comic (launched in 1950) – inspired a host of toys and spin-offs that are popular today.
Radio Station **£70–80**
Gun **£40–45**

▼ In 1947 two old school friends Leslie Smith and Rodney Smith, both discharged from the navy, joined forces and combined Christian names to create Lesney Products. The aim of the company was to produce simple and affordable diecast toys for children. In 1953 they devised their famous Matchbox range, inspired by the child of a company member who was only allowed to take playthings to school that were small enough to fit into a matchbox, hence the name and packaging. Matchbox vehicles were fun and affordable: "I could buy them with my own pocket money", remembers one nostalgic adult. "They were cheaper than a Corgi or Dinky, about the same price as the most basic Airfix kits, and they fitted perfectly in your pocket." All the Matchbox vehicles shown below date from the 1950s.

Boxed **£15–20** Unboxed **£10–15**

"...they fitted perfectly in your pocket"

▶ The 1950s saw a massive expansion in car ownership in Britain, along with the introduction of parking meters and the unveiling of the first motorway. Adult interest in cars was reflected in children's toys. On this Remote Control Driving Test game by Merit, vehicles were guided around the streets by use of a magnetic gear stick. Its good condition is probably due to the fact that the game looked better than it worked.

£20–30

◀ Pelham Puppets was launched by Bob Pelham in 1947. Hand-painted wooden puppets ranged from traditional models such as this witch to Disney characters. Known as "PelPop", Pelham wanted to encourage children to take up puppetry, and at its peak, his "Pelpup Club" had a membership of thousands. Puppets from the 1950s came in brown cardboard boxes, later replaced by yellow containers.

£20–30

▶ This selection of 1950s cars includes a Packard Clipper Sedan (with box) and a VW saloon by Dinky; and a Minic tinplate ambulance and a Hillman Husky by Corgi. These models were more expensive than the pocket-money Matchbox toys. Corgi was launched in 1956 to compete with the long established Dinky line, offering such seductively realistic innovations as plastic windows, rubber threaded tyres and spring suspension, gimmicks soon adopted by their rivals.

Packard Clipper **£50–60**

Ambulance **£40–60**   *VW & Corgi* **£15–20**

Rock and Pop

Rock 'n' roll is perhaps the most famous product of the 1950s. American teenagers tuned into radio stations playing "race" music: rhythm and blues and rock 'n' roll. The term rock 'n' roll (black slang for sex) was popularized by disc jockey Alan Freed. Black artists created the music; white singers introduced rock 'n' roll to an international audience. Bill Haley's *Rock Around the Clock* set teenagers dancing in cinemas around the world, while adults anguished about juvenile delinquency. Elvis Presley had twelve no.1 hits, before being drafted in 1958. He pioneered the image of the rock 'n' roll star as sex symbol and was filmed on television from the waist upward lest his gyrating pelvis corrupted American youth. A new archetype was created for the popular singer: the boy from the wrong side of town who looked mean, sang loud, lived hard and died young. The music of the 1950s is still popular and many still live out their fantasies as teddy boys and rockabillies. Rock and pop collectables can command high prices. With records condition is crucial to value, all the examples here are in mint condition.

◀ Elvis is among the most mythologized of all rock stars. Fans have even preserved his nail clippings and nothing is more desirable than an object that belonged to the King. Elvis wore this shirt in the 1957 film of *Jailhouse Rock;* it retains a studio label inscribed with his name. The shirt was originally won in a competition held by the magazine *Mirabelle* in 1957. *The Best of Elvis* (HMV) is from the same period.

Record **£150–175**

Shirt **£3000–4000**

◀▼ Dating from 1956, *Blue Jean Bop!* (EMI Capitol Records) was Gene Vincent's first album. He was famous for *Be Bop a Lul*a, his limp (result of a motorbike accident), his drinking and live shows of demonic energy. *Singin' to my Baby* (London Records, 1958) was the first album by Eddie Cochran. If Vincent was the "wild one", then Cochran was the James Dean of rock 'n' roll. On a British tour in 1960, their car crashed leaving Vincent badly injured and Cochran dead at the age of 21. His posthumous release was *Three Steps to Heaven*.

£75–100 *Each*

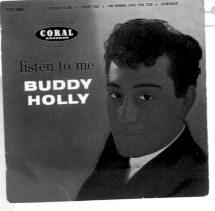

◄ Although Buddy Holly died at 22, he had been performing since the age of five. He created a host of rock classics from *That'll Be the Day* (no. 1 in 1957) to *It Doesn't Matter Any More*, released after the plane crash that killed Holly in February 1959. The EP record *Listen To Me* includes *Listen To Me*, *Peggy Sue*, *I'm Gonna Love You Too* and *Everyday*. The cover showing Holly without his trademark glasses was quickly withdrawn because Holly didn't like the naked image; it is very rare and highly collectable today.

Glasses on **£15–20** Glasses off **£275–300**

► Fat, thirty and married with five children, Bill Haley was an unlikely spearhead of teenage revolution. Nevertheless, the success of *Rock Around the Clock* in 1955 inspired an eponymous film and made Bill Haley and his Comets world famous. They enjoyed a string of hits over the next two years, from *See You Later Alligator* to *Rip It Up*. In 1957 they became the first rock 'n' roll band to tour abroad: "Oh man, we really are hoping to dig you British cats", Haley told the *Daily Mirror*. The album *Rock the Joint!* was released by London Records that same year.

£75–100

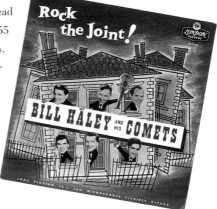

◄ Billy Ward founded the Dominoes in 1950. Featuring Clyde McPhatter, this extremely rare "doo-wop" record dates from 1956. "Doo-wop" describes the harmony singing popularized in the United States in the 1950s by both by black and Italian-American bands, including Dion and The Belmonts. Dion DiMucci's hits include *I Wonder Why* and *Teenager In Love*.

Dion **£150–175** Billy Ward **£1000–1500**

► Thanks to Carl Perkins, the ultimate item of rock 'n' roll apparel became a pair of blue suede shoes. Carl Perkins created the rock anthem in 1955. According to rumour, he wrote it on the back of a paper bag and it was inspired by Johnny Cash who suggested the line "Don't step on my blue suede shoes". This album was released by Sun Records in 1957. Perkins later returned to a fashion theme with *Pink Pedal Pushers* and *Pointed Toe Shoes*, songs that failed to equal the stature of his great footwear classic.

£75–100

"Don't step on my blue suede shoes"

◄ Both of these EPs (extended play records) were released by London Records (1956–7), the discs themselves bearing London's distinctive and highly desirable gold label. Born Elias Bates in 1928, Bo Diddley gained his stage name in the boxing ring and was to use it consistently in his lyrics. He is best known for the distinctive "hambone" rhythm that he developed on his custom-made rectangular guitar, a pumping beat that Diddley describes in words as "Shave-and-a-haircut-six-bits". Chuck Berry is one of the seminal figures of rock history, drawing his influences both from rhythym and blues and country music ("the only Maybellene I ever knew was the name of a cow", he once claimed) and targeting his songs brilliantly at the 1950s teenage market.

£125–150 *Each*

"Shave-and-a-haircut-six-bits"

► Jazz was another 1950s favourite, appealing to an audience that was more self-consciously sophisticated than teen-oriented rock 'n' roll. The innovative "bop" sounds of Charlie Parker and Dizzy Gilliespie became the music of the Beat generation. This album *New Orleans Jazz* (1957) features Louis Armstrong, one of the greatest figures in jazz history. Compared to rock 'n' roll, some period jazz records can seem low in price. For jazz enthusiasts, listening to the music is more important than the rarity of an original record, and releases of old material on CD have affected values in the second-hand market.

£12–15

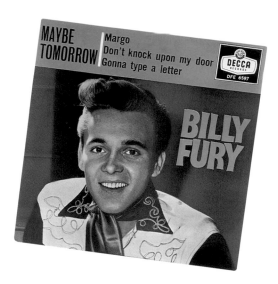

▲ American rock 'n' roll was hugely popular in Britain, inspiring a host of teenagers to pick up guitars and change their names to ones more likely to attract a teenage audience. Harry Webb became Cliff Richard, England's answer to Elvis Presley. The press attacked his "indecent" hip-swinging performances and success was assured. This is the album of the film *Expresso Bongo*, made in 1959 and starring Cliff as a bongo player, beating a path down Tin Pan Alley. Billy Fury (born Ronald Wycherly in 1941) was one of a stable of stars named and managed by successful pop promoter Larry Parnes. In 1959 Fury shot into the Top 20 with *Maybe Tomorrow*. Released by Decca, this orange-topped EP is extremely rare.

Cliff Richard **£12–15** *Billy Fury* **£100–125**

◄Brigitte Bardot poses with her husband, French actor Jacques Charrier, and singer Dalida in front of a jukebox, at the premiere of the musical show *Jukebox* at the Paris Etoile Theatre in 1959. Jukeboxes gave post-war teenagers the freedom to choose what music could be played in public. Today jukeboxes are seen as icons of popular culture and are highly collectable. Prices depend on decorative appeal (Art Deco designs are sought after), working condition, restoration and whether a dealer offers a guarantee. This jukebox is a Seeburg model L 200, dating from 1959.

£2500–3000

Film

Cinema audiences peaked in the 1940s but by the 1950s audiences were down and cinemas were competing with television. Hollywood fought back with lavish epics boasting casts of thousands and costs of millions, and such new technology as 3D and Cinerama, the wide-screen effect developed during the war to provide combat simulation for pilots. In America young people were attracted to drive-in cinemas by teen and horror B-movies shown in triple bills that gave their audience plenty of time to neck in the back of the chevy. Marlon Brando and James Dean were the inarticulate rebel heroes of this new teenage generation. Female stars offered more paradoxical role models, ranging from the girl-next-door type portrayed by Doris Day, to the blond and busty sex goddess epitomized by Marilyn Monroe, to the ladylike elegance of stars such as Audrey Hepburn and Grace Kelly, the screen princess who married a real life prince.

Film memorabilia from the 1950s is highly sought after and can now fetch extremely high prices. Enthusiasts specialize both in individual stars and particular genres, horror and science fiction being current favourites.

Day by Day · DORIS DAY

◄ "I've been around so long, I knew Doris Day before she was a virgin", ran a Hollywood joke attributed to Groucho Marx. In a world populated by sex sirens, Doris Day's image was wholesome and ordinary, the kind of girl more likely to wear Peter Pan collared pyjamas to bed than a "Monroesque" dab of Chanel No. 5. Correspondingly, she attracts fewer collectors than her more glamorous contemporaries. The album *Day by Day* was released by Philips *c.*1957.

£25–35

"I've been around so long, I knew Doris Day before she was a virgin"

◄► Made in 1957 by Poynter Products, USA, this hard plastic, moulded hot-water bottle allowed purchasers to claim that they had slept with Jayne Mansfield. The American tie, plain and innocent from the front, conceals her portrait in the lining. Jayne Mansfield (b.1933) was the ultimate blonde bombshell. Although her acting talents were limited, her talent for self-publicity was endless and with measurements of 40in (101cm) bust, 18½in (47cm) waist, and 36in (91cm) hips, her film assets are obvious. Mansfield was decapitated in a sports car accident in 1967, leaving behind a selection of largely indifferent films and a wealth of desirable memorabilia.

Hot-water bottle **£70–90**

Tie **£150–200**

◄With their high quality and dramatic artwork, Italian film posters are greatly prized by collectors. These two posters, *Fronte del Porto (On the Waterfront,* 1954) and *Gioventu Bruciata (Rebel Without a Cause,* 1955), were designed respectively by Anselmo Ballester (1897–1974) and Luigi Martinati (1893–1984), two of the leading artists in the field. Film posters were only leased to cinemas; once returned to the distributors they were often destroyed, hence their value and rarity today. Since posters tended to be folded rather than rolled, many need restoration. These posters celebrate two of the most significant films and stars of the decade. Each poster measures 79 x 55in (200 x 140cm).

Gioventu Bruciata **£1400–1700** *Fronte del Porto* **£1700–2000**

►Born Norma Jean Baker in 1926, Marilyn Monroe has perhaps inspired more fascination and adulation than any other film star. Her career peaked in the 1950s and ended with her tragic suicide in 1962. Film magazines from the period tend to be inexpensive; however, if they have Marilyn on the cover they command a substantial premium. The 1950s examples illustrated here include *66: A Souvenir Album of Marilyn Photographs, Photoplay, Movieland* and *Modern Screen. Sunbathing Review* (Fall, 1958), from the American publishers of the *Nudist's Year Book,* promises uncensored pictures of Marilyn naked and is as such highly collectable. Any memorabilia associated with Marilyn commands very high prices.

£50–75 *Each*

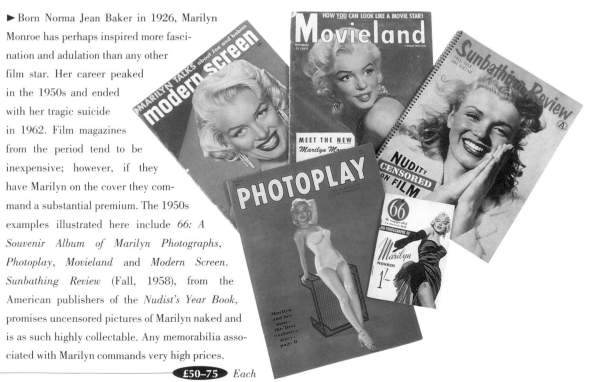

◄▼ These toys come from Walt Disney's *Peter Pan* (1953) and *Lady and the Tramp* (1955). Disney launched his hugely popular *Disneyland* television series in 1954. The show provided a perfect opportunity for promoting his films, merchandise and his amusement park, which opened in California (1955). A mass of "Disneyana" was made during the 1950s. Manufactured by Louis Marx, Disneykins were inexpensive plastic party favours made in Hong Kong. Peter Pan is only ½in (12mm) high. It is rare to find one in mint condition; unboxed it would be worth considerably less. The rubber dogs are from *Lady and the Tramp;* Scamp is unmarked while the Tramp was made by Walt Disney products (France).

Rubber models **£35–45** *Disneykins* **£20–30**

► This American poster for *Roman Holiday* (1953) measures 42 x 27in (107 x 68cm). The story of a princess (Audrey Hepburn) who falls in love with a reporter (Gregory Peck) gained added piquancy from coinciding with the romance of Princess Margaret and Peter Townsend. In 1951 Hepburn was spotted by Colette in a hotel lobby and was catapulted to Broadway stardom in *Gigi*. "After so many drive-in waitresses becoming movie stars... along comes class", approved the director William Wyler, who signed her for *Roman Holiday*.

£550–650

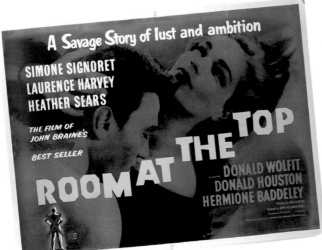

◄Published in 1957, John Braine's "scorching bestseller", *Room at the Top*, chronicled the loss of innocence and the rise to riches of ambitious working-class lad, Joe Lampton. This is the poster for the film adaptation (1958) which starred Laurence Harvey and Simone Signoret. The film was notable both for its frank sensuality and its realistic portrayal of the vicious constraints of provincial life, reflecting interest in the working-class hero and the new social mobility. The poster measures 40 x 30in (101 x 76cm).

£300–350

► *The Fly* (1958) chronicles the adventures of a scientist who invents a disintegration machine and accidentally swaps his molecular pattern with a fly. "Help me! Help me!" cries the half-man half-fly. Filmed in Cinerama, *The Fly* not only demonstrates the contemporary fear and fascination with science fiction but also the taste for new cinematic gimmicks. This British poster of *The Fly* by Jock Hinchcliff measures 30 x 40in (76 x 101cm). Posters in the science fiction genre are highly collectable today.

£700–1000

"Help me! Help me!"

◄This is the American poster for *Baby Doll* (1956), directed by Elia Kazan and starring Carroll Baker as the film's child bride. Like Vladimir Nabokov's 1955 novel *Lolita*, the film focused on perhaps the most disturbing female archetype of the 1950s, the sexually precocious young woman. On a lighter note, the film also introduced the fashion for shortie "baby doll" night wear. The poster measures 41 x 27in (104 x 68cm).

£150–250

► Although the film company closed down in 1955, Ealing Studios nevertheless managed to produce some of the best British comedies of the decade. *The Lavender Hill Mob* (1951) starred Alec Guinness as a meek and mild English bank clerk who forges a brilliantly bizarre scheme to rob his employers. This poster was created by illustrator Ronald Searle (of St Trinians fame) and S. John Woods. It measures 41 x 27in (104 x 68cm). A larger example, with slightly different Searle artwork, made a world record auction price of £6,187 for a British film poster when sold in London in March 1995.

£1600–2000

Books and Magazines

If rock 'n' roll provided one form of youthful rebellion, then literature provided another. In the United States, Jack Kerouac coined the term "Beat" to describe a new generation of writers who embraced sex, drugs, travel and an improvised literary style matching the beat of jazz. In Britain, John Osborne's seminal play *Look Back in Anger* (1956) inspired the description "angry young man", which was applied to authors ranging from Kingsley Amis to John Braine, whose provincial working-class heroes exposed a corrupt establishment. Some wanted to change the world, others to escape from it. The 1950s saw Mills & Boon promoting their successful romances, a burgeoning pulp fiction market, and stories of crime, spies and suspense, led by super agent, James Bond. Entry into another world altogether was offered by science fiction, which reflected modern fear and fascination with space and scientific discovery. Many post-war writers are still affordable today. The price ranges given here depend on rarity, condition and the presence of a dust jacket.

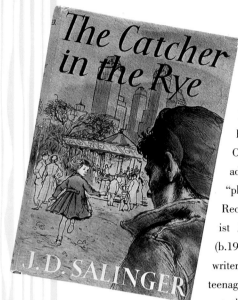

◄One of the cult books of the decade was *The Catcher in the Rye* (Hamish Hamilton, 1951). The hero of the book, 16-year-old Holden Caulfield, is a sensitive adolescent ill at ease in a "phoney" adult world. Reclusive American novelist Jerome David Salinger (b.1919) was among the first writers to focus on the sense of teenage unrest and disillusionment that manifested itself in various forms throughout the 1950s. The cover of this English first edition was designed by Fritz Wegner.

£250–300

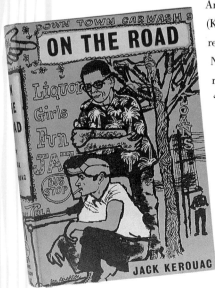

▼ "Liquor, Girls, Fun, Jazz" boasts the cover of Jack Kerouac's *On the Road* (Andre Deutsch, 1958). Written in the space of a few weeks and on a single continuous roll of teletype paper for the sake of speed and spontaneous flow, *On the Road* was the great novel of the Beat generation. Partly a *roman à clef*, it tells of the questing journey through America of Sal Paradise (Kerouac), Dean Moriarty (his real-life friend and mentor Neil Cassady), and a group of restless young Americans "mad to live, mad to talk, mad to be saved". This novel has never lost its romantic appeal and is highly collectable today. A first American edition can be worth more than twice as much as this British first edition.

£400–500

► At the age of 43, and to take his mind off his impending marriage, Ian Fleming wrote his first novel in only eight weeks. He wanted a dull name for his hero. *Birds of the West Indies* was a favourite book and the name of its author, James Bond, seemed a perfect choice. *Casino Royale* was published in 1953, the first of many Bond novels to be typed on Fleming's gold-plated typewriter. The books shown include the first paperback edition of *Casino Royale* (Pan Books, 1955) and the hardback edition of *Live and Let Die* (Jonathan Cape, 1954).

— *Live & Let Die* **£600–700** *Casino Royale* **£40–50**

◄ *Absolute Beginners* by Colin MacInnes (MacGibbon & Kee, 1959) celebrates the teenage scene in 1950s London. He conjures up a world of race riots, jazz dives and teddy boys, where slick youths in sharp Italian suits burst from the underclass to confound "the Oldies" and take the city by storm. Although the price range reflects the poor condition of this book, values for MacInnes and other key British writers of the period (John Braine, Alan Sillitoe) remain comparatively low and can provide an interesting and affordable area for collectors. Kingsley Amis is the most collectable of the "angry young men" and a first edition of *Lucky Jim* could be worth *c.*£1,000.

£25–35

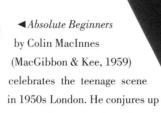

► With their lurid covers, pulp fiction novels from the 1950s and early 1960s are attracting a growing number of collectors. These paperbacks often took American themes. British writer Hank Janson (born Stephen Daniel Frances in 1917) chose his first name because it sounds like Yank. He specialized in pseudo American gangster stories and wrote some 300 novels with sales approaching 20 million. "Hank Janson Addicts need not be told that the man is a crime reporter with a flair for mixing it with super criminals and superb women", boasts the blurb on *Beloved Traitor*. John Creasey penned over 500 novels; *No Darker Crime* was published in 1959.

£2–5 *Each*

◄The post-war years saw the burgeoning of the girlie magazine industry which was led by the United States. In December 1953 Hugh Hefner launched *Playboy* magazine. He was so uncertain of success that he didn't even date the first issue in case there wasn't a second. By 1957 print runs were approaching one million. Britain lagged far behind its glamorous American rivals. *Spick* (1953) and its sister publication *Span* (1954) shown here were pocket-sized magazines aimed at the lowest end of the market. As their names suggest, they were tame, with modest poses and much airbrushing.

£3–5 *Each*

▼ *Mediterranean and French Country Food* (1951) was one of many books by the writer who revolutionized British home cooking. Into a world of rationing Elizabeth David (1912-22) brought the flavour, colour and smell of the Mediterranean. "Even if people could not very often make the dishes," she wrote, "it was stimulating to escape from the deadly boredom of queuing.... to read about real food cooked with wine and olive oil." The cover was designed by John Minton.

£10–15

◄Born in Russia in 1920, the American scientist Isaac Asimov was one of the great science fiction writers. In the collection of stories *I, Robot* (Grayson and Grayson, 1952) Asimov developed his "Laws of Robotics", showing robots as creatures responsible to man, servants and allies of the human race.

£80–175

▶ *Decorative Art, The Studio Year Book* was an annual catalogue of the latest international trends in home furnishing. It focused on modern design, catering to the fashionable homeowner. These volumes date from the 1950s and are much sought after by collectors and dealers today, providing a useful source for identifying period objects.

£20–30 *Each*

▶ Magazines from the 1950s are still widely available and provide a fascinating source of contemporary social history. These copies of *Woman* and *Woman's Own* include: instructions for knitting a Coronation Beefeater, tips on dressing to impress the mother-in-law, and stern advice from agony aunts: "Is the shallow enjoyment of a good time worth the risk of losing your good name?"

£1–3 *Each*

"Is the shallow enjoyment of a good time worth the risk of losing your good name?"

▶ This British edition of the magazine *Astounding Science Fiction (*June 1951) is remarkable for an article on "Dianetics" by the infamous L. Ron Hubbard (1911–86), pulp fiction writer and founder of the Church of Scientology in 1954. In *Seduction of the Innocent* (1955), Dr Frederick Wertham rails against the corruption of youth by such magazines. Ironically his enraged tract is now sought after by science fiction enthusiasts. American first editions fetch twice as much as this British example. The comics listed by Wertham have added kudos in the market.

Magazine **£20–25** *Book* **£40–50**

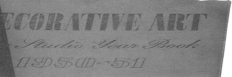

Useful Addresses

Where to buy

The following shops and dealers offer a range of collectable items from the 1950s. Markets and fairs are good hunting grounds too.

Alfies Antiques Market
13–25 Church Street
London NW8
1950s Dealers:
Antigo *Decorative arts*
Circle *Decorative arts*
Collector's World *Toys*
David Huxtable *Tins*
Ephemera & Packaging
Richard Gibbon *Costume jewellery*
Glassworks *Italian glass*
Francesca Martine *Jewellery*
& Decorative arts
Planet Bazaar *Post-war designs*
John Rastall *1950s Ceramics*
& Decorative arts
Geoffrey Robinson *Decorative arts*
Alvin Ross *Toys*

Atomic
34b Heathcote Street
Nottingham
Decorative arts & Kitchen appliances

Bayswater Books/Platinum
Age Comics
27a Craven Terrace
London W2

Linda Bee
Stand J20/21, Grays Antique Market,
1–7 Davies Mews
London W1Y
Costume jewellery, Bags & Compacts

The Beyst Jukebox Company
Muckton Bottom
Louth, Lincs

Century Design
68 Marylebone Road
London W1
Furniture & Decorative arts

Deco Inspired
67 Monmouth Street
London WC2
American furniture & Decorative arts

Design Goes Pop
34-36 Oldham Street
Manchester
20th-century design

Flying Duck Enterprises
320-322 Creek Road
Greenwich
London SE10
Post-war decorative arts

Gekoski
Pied Bull Yard
15a Bloomsbury Square
London WC1, *Books*

Ginnel Gallery
18–22 Lloyd Street
Manchester
Decorative arts

Harrington Bros
Chelsea Antiques Market
253 Kings Road
London SW3, *Books*

Maggs Brothers Limited
50 Berkeley Square
London W1
Books

Ed Mason
Shop 5, Chelsea Antiques Market
253 King's Road
London SW3
Film memorabilia

Memory Lane Records
55 Frith Road
Croydon, Surrey
Vintage records

New Century
69 Kensington Church Street
London W8
Decorative arts

On the Air
42 Bridge Street Row
Chester, Cheshire
Televisions and radios

Orsini Gallery
284 Portobello Road
London W10
Vintage clothing, open Fri. & Sat.

Rennies
13 Rugby Street
London WC1
Furniture & Decorative arts

The Reel Poster Company
First Floor
22 Great Marlborough Street
London W1
Movie posters

Rokit
225 Camden High Street
London NW1   (and at)
23 Kensington Gardens
Brighton
East Sussex
Vintage clothing

Sparkle at the Stables
Long Stables
Chalk Farm Road
Camden
London NW1
American fashions, open Sat. & Sun.

Sandy Stagg
282 Portobello Road
London W10
Vintage clothing, open Fri. & Sat.

Steinberg and Tolkein
193 Kings Road
London SW3
Vintage & designer clothing

Tom Tom
42 New Compton Street
London WC2
Post-war designs

Twentieth Century Design
274 Upper Street
London N1
Furniture & decorative arts

Twentieth Century Retro
166 Stoke Newington
Church Street
London N16
Vintage clothing

Ulysses Bookshop
31 & 40 Museum Street
London WC1
Books

The Vintage Magazine Co Ltd
39–43 Brewer Street
London W1
Magazines

Nigel Williams
22 & 25 Cecil Court
London WC2
Books

Markets

Portobello Market
Portobello Road
London W11
Open Fri. & Sat.

Camden Market
Chalk Farm Road
London NW1
Open Sat. & Sun.

Auction Houses

Bonhams
Montpelier Street,
Knightsbridge
London SW7

Christie's South Kensington
85 Old Brompton Road
London SW7

Sotheby's
34–5 New Bond Street
London W1

Select Bibliography

Ball, Joan Dubbs, *Costume Jewelers: The Golden Age of Design*, Schiffer, 1990

Banham, Mary and Hillier, Bevis, *Festival of Britain, A Tonic to the Nation*, Thames and Hudson, 1976

Barker, Patricia, *Fashions of a Decade, The 1950s*, B. T. Batsford, 1991

Becker, Vivienne, *Fabulous Fakes*, Grafton, 1988

Bennett Levy, Michael, *TV is King*, MBL Publications, 1994

Bishop, Christina, *Miller's Collecting Kitchenware*, Miller's, Reed Books, 1995

Black, J. Anderson and Garland, Madge, *A History of Fashion*, Orbis Publishing, 1975

Booker, Christopher, *The Necrophiliacs*, Collins, 1969

Burns, Mark and Di Bonis, Louis, *Fifties Homestyle*, Thames and Hudson, 1988

Carrington, Noel, *Design and Decoration in the Home*, B.T.Batsford, 1952

Chenoune, Farid, *A History of Men's Fashion*, Flammarion, 1993

Chipman, Jack, *Collector's Encyclopaedia of California Pottery*, Collector Books, Schroeder Publishing, 1992

Corson, Richard, *Fashions in Makeup*, Peter Owen, 1972

Daily Mail Ideal Home Book and *Decorative Art, The Studio Year Book* (annual publications in the 1950s)

Dooner, Kate E., *Plastic Handbags, Sculpture to Wear*, Schiffer, 1992

Dooner, Kate E., *A Century of Handbags, Sculpture to Wear*, Schiffer, 1993

Dormer, Peter, *Design Since 1945, Fifties Homestyle*, Thames and Hudson ,1993

Drake, Nicholas, *The Fifties in Vogue*, Henry, Holt and Company, Conde Nast Publications, 1987

Ettinger, Roseann, *50s Popular Fashions*, Schiffer, 1995

Ettinger, Roseann, *Forties and Fifties Popular Jewellery*, Schiffer, 1995

Ferragamo, Salvatore, *The Art of the Shoe*, Centro Di, 1987

Fiell, Charlotte & Peter, *Modern Chairs*, Taschen, 1993

Gabor, Mark, *The Pin-Up, A Modest History*, Andre Deutsch, 1972

Garner, Philippe, *Twentieth Century Furniture*, Phaidon, 1980

Gillett, Charlie, *The Sound of the City*, Sphere Books, 1971

Gibbings, Sarah, *The Tie*, Studio Editions,1990

Gordon, Angie, Twentieth *Century Costume Jewellery*, Adasia International 1990

Greenburg, Cara, *Mid-Century Modern, Furniture of the 1950s*, Thames and Hudson, 1995

Heiremans, Mark, *Art Glass from Murano*, 1993

Hiesinger, K.B and Marcus, G.H., *Landmarks of Twentieth Century Design*, Abbeville Press, 1993

Hillier, Bevis, *Austerity Binge, The Decorative Arts of the Forties and Fifties*, Studio Vista London, 1955

Hillier, Bevis, *The Style of the Century, 1900–1980*, The Herbert Press, 1986

Hine, Thomas, *Populuxe*, Bloomsbury, 1987

Hiort, Esbjorn, *Modern Danish Furniture*, Architectural Book Publishing Co., New York, 1956

Howell, Georgina, *In Vogue, Six Decades of Fashion*, Allen Lane, 1975

Jackson, Lesley, *Contemporary Architecture and Interiors of the 1950s*, Phaidon Press, 1994

Jackson, Lesley, *The New Look, Design in the Fifties*, Thames and Hudson 1991

Katz, Sylvia, *Classic Plastics*, Thames and Hudson, 1984

Larkin, Colin (ed), *The Guinness Encyclopaedia of Popular Music*, Guinness Publishing 1993

Lewis, Peter, *The Fifties*, Heinemann, 1978

MacCarthy, Fiona, *British Design Since 1880*, Lund Humphries, 1982

McDowell, Colin, *Hats*,Thames and Hudson, 1992

Marling, Karal Ann, *As Seen On TV, The Visual Culture of Everyday Life in the 1950s*, Harvard University Press, 1994

Marly, Diana de, *Christian Dior*, B. T. Batsford, 1990

Martin, Richard (ed), *Contemporary Fashion*, St James Press, 1996

Massey, Anne, *Interior Design of the 20th century*, Thames and Hudson, 1990

Mauries, Patrick, *Fornasetti, Designer of Dreams*, Thames and Hudson, 1991

Mentasti, Rosa Barovier, *Venetian Glass 1890–1990*, Arsenale Editrice, 1992

Moody, Ella, *New Century Gallery, Rye Pottery* (exhibition catalogue), London, 1996

Naylor, Colin (ed) *Contemporary Designers*, St James Press, 1990

Niblett, Kathy, *Dynamic Design, The British Pottery Industry 1940-1980*, Stoke-on-Trent Museum and Art Gallery, 1990

Opie, Jennifer, *Scandinavian Ceramics and Glass in the Twentieth Century*, Victoria & Albert Musum, 1989

Payton, Leland and Crystal, *Decorative Lamps of the Fifties*, Abbeville Press, 1989

Peat, Alan, *Midwinter A Collectors' Guide*, Cameron & Hollis, 1992

Philadelphia Museum of Art, *Design Since 1945*, Exhibition Catalogue, 1983

Polak, Ada, *Modern Glass*, Faber and Faber, 1962

Polhemus, Ted, *Street Style*, Thames and Hudson, 1995

Potter, Margaret & Alexander, *Interiors*, John Muray, 1957

Porter. Catherine, *Miller's Collecting Books*, Miller's, Reed Books, 1995

Probert, Christina, *Swimwear in Vogue*, Thames and Hudson, 1981

Schoeser, Mary, *Fabrics and Wallpapers, Twentieth Century Design*, Bell &Hyman, 1986

Schoeser, Mary and Rufey Celia, *English and American Textiles*, Thames and Hudson, 1989

Seymour-Smith, Martin, *Novels and Novelists*, St Martin's Press, 1980

Smith, Nigel, *Britain Since 1945*, Wayland Publishers, 1990

Sommer, Robert Langley, *Toys of our Generation*, Magana Books, 1992

Sparke, Penny, *Furniture, Twentieth-Century Design*, Bell & Hyman, 1986

Sparke, Penny, *Electrical Appliances, Twentieth Century Design*, Bell & Hyman, 1987

Steele, H. Thomas, *The Hawaiian Shirt*, Thames and Hudson, 1984

Stoneback, Bruce and Diane, *Matchbox Toys*, The Apple Press, 1993

The Studio magazine

Tames, Richard, *The 1950s*, Franklin Watts, 1990

Tibballs, Geoff, *The Guinness Book of Innovations*, Guiness Publishing, 1994

Trasko, Mary, *Heavenly Soles*, Abbeville, 1989

Vogue magazine, 1950s British editions

Wahlberg, Holly, *Everyday Elegance, 1950s Plastic Design*, Schiffer, 1994

Index

Page numbers in *italic*
refer to illustrations and
captions, those in **bold** to
main entries

143

Acknowledgments

The publisher and author would like to thank the following people for supplying pictures for use in the book or for allowing their pieces to be photographed.

Special thanks to Neil Bingham for his generosity and assistance, to Simon Alderson and Tony Cunningham for their advice, to Alexander Payne, Simon Andrews, Linda Bee, Gail Higgins, Wendy Gaye and the press offices at Bonhams and Christie's South Kensington.

Key

b bottom *c* centre
t top *l* left *r* right

(A) Alfies
(B) Bonhams
(C) Christie's S. Ken.
(Pop) Design Goes Pop
(DI) Deco Inspired
(FD) Flying Duck Enterprises
(G) Ginnels
(LB) Linda Bee
(ML) Memory Lane Records
(RPG) Reel Poster Gallery
(S) Sotheby's
(SM) Sparkle Moore
(20th) 20th Century Design
(ST) Steinbeck & Tolkien
(W) Wendy Gaye
(NB) Neil Bingham
(BB) Bayswater Bookshop

Photographers:
(IB) Ian Booth
(TR) Tim Ridley
(RS) Robin Saker

R © Reed International Books Limited

back jkt flap/front & back cover RIB (B); back jkt *br* R/IB (B); back jkt *cr* (TR) (M), back jkt *tr* R/IB (B); front jkt *br* R/IB (B); front jkt *bl* R/IB (B); front jkt *tl* (TR) (M) ; front jkt centre R/TR (FD); front jkt flap R/TR (SM); front jkt *tr* (TR) (M); back jkt *c* R/TR (M); **1** R/TR (FD); **2 /3** R/TR (FD); **4 /5** R/TR (FD); **8**Royle Publications Ltd ; **10** *l* R (Miller's); *l* R/RS (Miller's); **11** *l* R (Miller's), *r* R/Ken Adlard (Miller's); **12** *l* R/IB (A), *r* R/RS (DP); **13** *l* R/TR (20C), *r* (RPG) ; **14** Advertising Archives ; **16** *tl* R/TR (20C), *bl* R/TR (20C); **17** *tl* R/IB (C), *tr* R/TR (20C), *bl* R/IB (C), *br* R/IB (B); **18** *tl* R/TR (20C), *b* R/TR (20C), *tr* R/TR (20C); **19** *b* R (B), *t* R/TR (20C); **20** *t* R/IB (B), *b* R/IB (B); **21** *tl* R/IB (B), *r* R/IB (C), *bl* R/TR (NB); **22** *tl* (IB) (B), *bl* (B) (C), *br* R/IB (B); **23** *tl* (IB) (S), *tr* R/IB (B), *cl* R/IB (S), *br* R/IB (B), *b* R/IB (B); **24** *tr* R/IB (B), *b* R/IB (B); **25** *tr* R/IB (C), *c* R/TR (20C), *b* R/IB (A); **26** *b* R/TR (NB), *t* R/IB (C); **27** *tr* R/TR (NB), *c* R/IB (C), *b* R/IB (C); **28** *t* R/TR (DI), *b* R/TR (FD), **29** *t* R/TR (20C), *b* R/IB (C), *b* R/IB (S); **30** *t* R/TR (FD), *b* R/TR (FD); **31** *tr* R/TR (FD), *c* R/TR (NB), *b* R/TR (DI); **32** *t* Courtesy of G Plan Upholstery Ltd, *b* R/TR (NB); **33** *tl* R/TR (FD), *c* R/TR (SM), *bl* R/IB (C); **34** *tr* R/TR (FD), *bl* R/TR (SM), *br* R/TR (FD); **35** *t* R/TR (FD), *c* R/IB (C), *bl* R/TR (FD), *br* R/TR (FD); **36** *t* R/IB (B) *b* R/IB (C); **37** *t* R/IB (B), *bl* R/TR (20C), *br* R/IB (C); **38** *tr* R/TR (FD), *cl* R/TR (FD), *cr* R/TR (20C), *bc* R/TR (FD); **39** *t* R/TR (DI), *br* R/TR (DI); **40** *t* R/IB (On The Air), Hulton Getty Picture Collection; **41** *t* R/IB (S) *c* R/IB (On The Air), *b* R/TR (DI) ; **42** *t* R/RS (Pop), *tr* R/TR (FD), *c* R/IB (C), *b* R/TR (SM); **43** R (TR) (FD), *c* R/TR (FD), *b* R/TR (FD); **44** *t* Advertising Archives, R (RS) (Pop), *b* Sunbeam Corporation (Sunbeam and Mixmaster are registered trademarks of Sunbeam Corporation); **45** *t* R/RS (G), *tr* R/RS (Pop), *t* R/RS (Pop), *br* R/TR (FD); **46** *t* R/RS (Pop), *b* R/IB (A); **47** *tl* R/IB (C), *tr* R/RS (Pop), *cl* R/TR (M), *b* R/RS (Pop); **48** *t* R (RS) (G),*b* R/IB (B); **49** *t* R/TR (FD),*r* R/TR (M), *cl* R/TR (M), *b* R (Martin Norris/Chrisina Bishop); **50** background logo Successful Farming, Meredith Publishing Company, Des Moines, Iowa, *t* R/TR (FD), *b* R. (RS) (Pop), *br* R/RS (Pop); **51** *t* R/TR (DI), *cr* R/IB (A), *bl* R/IB (A); **52** *t* R/IB (A), *b* R/TR (DI); **53** R/TR (DI), *c* R/TR (DI), *b* R/TR (SM); **54** *t* R/TR (FD), *b* R/RS (G); **55** *t* R/TR (FD), *c* R/RS (G), *b* (IB) (C), *b* R/RS (Pop); **56** *t* R/TR (FD), *tl* R/TR (NB), *bl* R/TR (NB), *bc* R/IB (A), *br* R/TR (NB); **57** *tl* R/TR NB, *tc* R/RS (G), *tr* R/IB (A), *b* R/RS (G); **58** *tl* R/IB (A), *r* R/IB (A),*b* R/IB (New Century); **59** *tl* R/IB (A), *cr* R/TR (FD), *cl* R/TR (FD), *br* R/IB (Rennies); **60** R *t* (IB) (A), *c* (IB) (A), *b* R/IB (C); **61** *t* R/RS (G), *bl* R/RS (G), *br* R/RS (G); **62** *tl* R/IB (C),*c* R/IB (B), *b* R/IB (A); **63** *t* R/TR (NB), *bl* R/RS (Pop), *br* R/RS (G); **64** *t* R/IB (A), *b* R/IB (New Century), **65** *tl* Corning Museum of Glass, *tr* R/IB (A), *bl* R/IB (B),*br* R/IB (A); **66** *tr* R/IB (A), *bl* R/IB (A), *br* R/IB (A); **67** *t* R (RS) (G), *c* R/RS(G), *b* R/RS(G); **68** *t* R/IB (C), *b* R/IB (C); **69** *tl* R/IB (C), *tr* R/IB (C), *bl* R/IB (C), *br* R/IB (B); **70** *t* R/TR (FD), *c* R/TR (SM), *b* R/RS (Pop); **71** *tl* R/TR (SM), *tr* R/IB (A), *bl* R/RS(Pop), *br* R/TR (FD); **72** *t* R/IB (A), *b* R (TR) (NB); **73** *t* R (TR) (FD), *c* R/TR (FD), *b* R/TR (FD); **74** *t* R/TR (FD), *c* R/TR (FD), *b* R/TR (FD); **75** *t* R/TR (SM), *c* R/TR (FD), *b* R/TR (SM); **76** *t* R/RS (G), *b* C Images, *tl* R/IB (A); **77** *tr* R/IB (A), *bl* R/IB (A), *br* R/IB (A); **78** *tl* R/IB(B), *tr* R/TR (FD), *b* R/IB (B); **79** *t* R/TR (FD), *c* R/TR (FD), *b* R/IB (S); **80** *t* R/IB (B), *c* R/IB (C), *b* R/TR (FD), **81** *t* R/TR (FD), *c* R/IB (C), *b* R/IB (B); **82** *t* R/IB (C), *bl* R/IB (New Century), *br* R/TR (NB); **83** *tl* R/TR (DI), *c* R/TR (M), *br* R/TR (M); **84** Courtesy Vogue 4154 c1954 by The Conde Nast Publications; **86** *t* R/IB (LB), *b* R/TR (ST); **87** *t* R/TR (SM), *cr* R/TR (ST), *br* R/TR (ST); **88** *t* R/TR (SM), *b* R/TR (ST); **89** *t* R/TR (ST), *tr* R/TR (ST); *b* R/TR (ST); **90** *t* R/TR (SM), *bl* R/TR (SM), *br* R/TR (M); **91** *tl* R/TR (M), *c* R/TR (M), *b* R/TR (SM); **92** *tl* R/TR (ST), *c* R/TR (ST),*bl* R/TR (ST); **93** *tr* R/TR (ST), *c* R/TR (ST), *b* R/TR (M); **94** *tl* R/TR (SM), *tr* R/TR (SM), *b* R/TR (SM); **95** *tr* R/TR (SM), *c* R (RS) (20th Century Retro), *b* Rawlings *c* Conde Nast Pl Vogue; **96** *t* R/TR (SM), *b* R/TR (SM); **97** *tl* R/TR (SM), *c* R/TR (SM), *b* R/TR (SM); **98** *t* R/TR (SM), *c* R/TR (SM), *b* R/TR (SM); **99** *t* R (TR) (SM), *b* (TR) (SM); **100** *t* R/TR (ST), *b* R (RS) (20th Century Retro); **101** *t* R/TR (SM), *c* R (IB) (Rennies), *b* R/RS (ST); **102** *t* R/TR (LB), *b* R/TR (LB), **103** *tr* R/TR (LB), *c* R/TR (SM), *br* R/TR (LB); **104** *t* R/TR (ST), *b* R/TR (LB); **105** *tr* R/TR (LB), *t* (IB) (Rennies), *b* R/TR (SM); **106** *tl* R/TR (LB), *t* R/TR (LB), *b* R/TR (LB); **107** *r* R/TR (LB), *c* R/TR (LB), *br* R/TR (SM);**108** *tl* R/IB (A), *b* R (IB) (A);**109** *tr* R/IB (A), *cl* R/IB (A), *br* R/TR (A); **110** *tl* R/TR (LB), *cr* R/TR (LB), *bl* R/TR (SM), *t* R/TR (SM); **111** *b* R/IB (A); **112** *t* R/TR(SM), *b* R/TR (SM); **113** *tr* R/TR (SM), *cl* R/TR (SM), *b* Hulton Getty Picture Collection ; **114** *t* R/IB (Rokit), *b* R/RS (20th Century Retro); **115** *t* R/TR (SM), *br* R/TR (SM); **116** *t* R/TR (SM), *c* R/RS (20th Century Retro), *b* R/RS (?); **117** *tl* R/RS (20th Century Retro), *b* R/RS (20th Century Retro), *tr* R/RS (20th Century Retro); **118** Redferns (Glenn A Baker Archives); **120** *t* R/IB (A),*b* R/IB (Sue Pearson); **121** *tr* R/IB (A), *cl* R/IB (A), *br* R/TR (B); **122** *t* R/IB (A), *b* R/IB (A); **123** *tr* R/IB (A), *c* R/IB (A), *b* R/IB (A); **124** *tr* R/IB (ML), *tl* R/IB (Philips, London), *b* R/IB (ML), *b* R (ML); **125** *t* R/IB (ML), *c* R/IB (ML), *b* R/IB (ML); **126** *tr* R/IB (ML), *c* R/IB (ML), *b* R/IB (ML); **127** *tl* R/IB (private collection), *tr* R/IB (ML), *b* Corbis-Bettmann (UPI); **128** *t* R/IB (ML), *bl* R/IB (W), *br* R/TR (SM); **129** *tr* (RPG), *tl* (RPG), *b* R/IB (W); **130** *tl* R/IB (A), *c* (RPG), *c* (RPG), *b* (RPG) ; **131** *t* (RPG), *l* (RPG), *b* (RPG) ; **132** *t* R/IB (Nigel Williams), *b* (Ulysses bookshop) ; **133** *t* R/IB (BB), *c* (Maggs Bookshop), *b* R /IB (BB); **134** *t* R/IB (A), *c* (Ken Adlard), *bl* R (Books For Cooks), *br* R/TR (M); **135** *t* R/TR (M), *r* R/IB (BB)